T0355540

Business Strategy

Plan, Execute, Win!

Patrick J. Stroh

WILEY

Published by John Wiley & Sons, Inc., Hoboken, New Jersey.
Published simultaneously in Canada.

For general information on our other products and services or for technical support, please
contact our Customer Care Department within the United States at (800) 762-2974,
outside the United States at (317) 572-3993 or fax (317) 572-4002.

Wiley publishes in a variety of print and electronic formats and by print-on-demand.
Some material included with standard print versions of this book may not be included
in e-books or in print-on-demand. If this book refers to media such as a CD or DVD
that is not included in the version you purchased, you may download this material at
http://booksupport.wiley.com. For more information about Wiley products, visit
www.wiley.com.

Library of Congress Cataloging-in-Publication Data:

Stroh, Patrick J., 1969-
    Business strategy : *plan, execute, win* / Patrick J. Stroh.
        pages   cm
        ISBN 978-1-118-87844-6 (hardback) — ISBN 978-1-118-89321-0 (ePDF) —
    ISBN 978-1-118-89322-7 (ePub)   1. Strategic planning.   2. Leadership.   I. Title.
    HD30.28.S77 2014
    658.4'012—dc23

                                                                                          2014003247

Printed in the United States of America
10 9 8 7 6 5 4 3 2 1

Contents

Contents v

Preface

The original working title of this book was "The 'S' Word: Parables on Business Strategy." It ended up being revised to the current title, *Business Strategy: Plan, Execute, Win!*, but the origination of that first title sets some interesting context for the introduction of this book. Business Strategy is important; few senior executives and CEOs would disagree with that. So if it is important, why does "strategy" have a bad reputation in many companies and circles of executives? In the original title, the play on title was that "S" stood for strategy, but there are some who think it stands for another "S" word; you know, the four-letter profanity. Well, it could just as well be that sometimes.

It seems that the concept, function, and consulting around "strategy" has fallen so far from grace that the word "strategy" could be considered a four-letter profanity. Again, it's not that leaders don't agree that a strategy is needed and critical to achieve success, but they have gone through too many exercises and experiences where a five-year strategic plan was painfully created over six months with exercises like "If you were a tree, what type of tree would you be?" (That was a serious example.) Some executives may equate the pain of going through a strategic planning process akin to implementing an enterprise resource planning (ERP) system in a manufacturing environment. Many executives have war stories of the increased time and cost of implementing a new system, how the "synergies" didn't really pan out as expected and how many of the touted features were postponed.

Strategic planning in businesses, if done poorly, can feel the same way. You can go into the process feeling good, "Boy, are we going to sit down and really debate our strategy finally. I have a lot of ideas I want to get on the table. I want to look at some new product lines and maybe an acquisition or two." Then, reality sets in. Finance tells you what the "corporate template" needs to include for your submission to them. A customer is having an issue that needs immediate resolution so you're going to have to miss the first two planning sessions. Then, the healthy, strategic debate you expected turns into a round robin free-for-all of ideas, but no structure as to what to do with them, how to evaluate them, or what to explore further, and, worse yet, an all-out verbal lashing with two of your peers. Possibly then, the sessions are shelved, and you go back to "last year's plan" and simply make some updates. What a depressing process. It doesn't have to work this way, but all too often it does. Hence why it's the "S" word at some companies.

Tune in to station WIIFM – WIIFM, "What's in it for me? Ok, I get it you say, but do you want to spend part of your most precious resource, your time, to read more? Why? What should you hope to take away from this book?" Who was this really written for? I wouldn't promise to give you that one, singular, secret process or golden rule that works for all companies around business strategy, and since there is not one, I will promise to give you some golden nuggets in creating, applying, and executing business strategy. I am writing this book to share 20-plus years of experience in this space. I am NOT writing this book as a Harvard Business Case Review (nothing wrong with those; actually I really enjoy them), but I want this to be more of a "practitioner's guide" from a practitioner's viewpoint. Think of this book like a fireside chat with Roosevelt. The fireside chats were a series of 30 evening radio addresses given by U.S. President, Franklin D. Roosevelt between 1933 and 1944. This was not about politics; this was about Roosevelt simply telling the people

what he was doing and why. This style and level of inti-
macy with him made people feel as if they too were
part of the administration's decision-making process
and many soon felt that they knew Roosevelt personally and, most importantly, they grew to trust him.
I hope that over the course of reading this book, you
come to trust me and are intrigued with the discussion.
More important, I hope you learn from my learnings,
accelerate your business strategy through good practices,
and avoid the pitfalls that I have encountered. As far as
who would benefit most, we are aiming at the C-suite
or those that strive to be there:

- Those currently in the C-suite: Refreshers are good,
  right? Finding another viewpoint and comparing
  it and possibly melding it to your own is helpful,
  right? It's wise to seek counsel and advice from time
  to time, right? Hard to argue with these questions.
  If you have been around the block a time or two,
  many of these stories may elicit a grin on your face
  or a head nodding or a "been-there-before" lesson learned of your own. Others may elicit deeper
  thought and contemplation or simply serve as a
  reminder from your own experiences. Any way you
  look at it, "sharpening the saw" a bit, in Stephen
  Covey's terms, whether it's improving yourself or
  simply recharging, is usually a fruitful exercise, and
  you may find some new insights or aspects you have

not run into yet, or a new favorite process or tool to test out.

- Those aspiring to the C-suite: I think that through reading these stories and lessons learned, you can accelerate your learning in the discipline of business strategy, but it's not as simple as learning, say, one functional area in a company. You have to know a great deal about everything in your company, industry, and environment, or else you set strategy blindly. While you won't instantly be an expert and you will need to have your own "crucible moments" of learning, which by the way come both in successes and failures, you will have elevated your thinking and knowledge. Consider this a partial "executive MBA" in business strategy and a look into how senior executives view, plan, execute, and monitor strategy.

This book has been written purposely to a length of a three-to-four-hour plane ride, and it won't add ten pounds to your bag if you have a hardcopy. I travel a good deal, probably like you, and I'd rather have an informative, entertaining, "light" book in my bag to read on the onboard leg of a trip to psych myself up, or on the return leg to rejuvenate myself. Is investing one plane ride in yourself worth it? I think so, so get comfortable, adjust your pillow, and settle into these pages.

Learning Style—Parables—I am a big proponent of learning via storytelling. Especially in today's day and age, with Google, Bing, and other search engines at your fingertips, memorizing facts and figures is an archaic learning style. But the learning style of storytelling, while thousands of years old, is as applicable as ever. You'll find that this book is a collection of parables. Defined by www.dictionary.com, a parable is a short tale that illustrates a universal truth, one of the simplest of narratives. It sketches a setting, describes an action, and shows the results.

1. A short allegorical story designed to illustrate or teach some truth, religious principle, or moral lesson.
2. A statement or comment that conveys a meaning indirectly by the use of comparison, analogy, or the like.

This is the style of I have chosen to convey these lessons learned and thoughts around business strategy, its creation, application, and execution.

Ideas that Stick—Another premise of this book is retention. What good is reading a book that, when you finish it, you say, "That was great. I'll have to remember that," then you don't. I'm hoping that through the storytelling aspect, some of these ideas will better "stick" in your memory. A great book on this concept is *Made to Stick*. One of the best examples from this book talking about creating visual pictures versus facts is from the movie *Armageddon*. An over-caffeinated, stuttering scientist is trying to describe to the President of the United States the size of the asteroid that is about to obliterate the Earth via a figure of square miles and size that is incomprehendible. The President isn't getting it, so the scientist's boss steps in. "The asteroid is the size of Texas, Mr. President." Now that sticks!

Gold Nuggets—At the end of every chapter, you'll find a conclusions section that will prompt you to consider, based on the chapter you've just read, to write down two "gold nuggets you took away to share with your board of directors or your staff, or for personal reflection." Remember taking notes in college? Taking notes helps with retention. And listing only a couple of nuggets forces you to reflect and prioritize what you just read. But don't just list the nuggets and stop, share these nuggets with your board of directors, your staff, your team, whomever makes sense, or take a couple away for later personal reflection. If the nuggets stay in your book, they don't advance any strategies; use them! I don't anticipate every story will have an ah-ha moment or learning, but over the course of a chapter, you should at least be able to reflect on two gold nuggets to take away for yourself and to share with others.

Business Strategy/Leadership/General Management—Early readers of this book gave good feedback on the book, style, and insights, but questioned, "Is this a book about business strategy or is it a book about leadership and general management? Because I feel the examples and insights apply to both." My response: I wholeheartedly agree—business strategy, leadership, and general management are all inextricably linked, or at least should be. Much of the advice and insights you read about what it takes to be a great leader is similar to what you'll read about how to be successful with business strategy. I can't prove this via a mathematical proof, but I can attest to it through experience. Strategy starts at the top, as does leadership and general management rules of engagement in a business. Good leaders understand strategy and good strategists need to be good leaders and understand what it takes to be a good manager else their strategic plans can be flawed and unobtainable. Therefore, as you read this book, be attentive that business strategy, leadership, and general management are all inextricably tied together and all are needed in unison to be successful in business strategy creation and execution.

Acknowledgments

I'd like to thank a number of people for helping me get this work to see the light of day.

Thanks to some of my early editors and advisors who proofed early versions, offered their opinions for improvements, honestly and gently, and gave me encouragement multiple times. Thanks to Jerry O, Alice D, Vicky C, Ben S, Phillip S, Dan K, Pat H, Meredith B, and Neil O.

Thanks to my mentors and prior leaders, who I have enjoyed working with and learning from—part of the success I've had is because I paid attention to what you said and did, even when you didn't know I was looking: Jackie K, Jim H, Ken H, John W, John S, David S, Todd B, and my parents.

Thanks to Jeff T and Greg B for their guidance and advice on publishing choices, process, and partners.

Thanks to Wiley, and specifically to Sheck C, who helped make this process as painless as possible and guided me through the publishing process.

Thanks to my personal chief editor and sounding board, my wife, Michelle, who listened to so many stories, read so many versions, and bit her lip when I repeated myself for the twentieth time telling a story.

Thanks to my kids, Alex, Rachel, and Jake, for inspiring me and encouraging me to write this book, which I've wanted to do for some time. I see them excel in high school and college and I aspire to learn like they do—persistently and relentlessly every day.

To anyone I have mistakenly omitted, please accept my apologies. There is no shortage of people whom I respect, seek the counsel of, and whose ears I bend from time to time—thank you!

Part I

LEVEL SETTING/ FOUNDATION

Part I of this book is a baseline for Parts II and III. I will set some context and give a little perspective on how strategic planning needs and processes have evolved and what the role should be for a person who is responsible for strategy today. Many companies have created and hired positions now for chief strategy officers (CSOs). I myself was a chief strategy and innovation officer in a Fortune 20 company. I have some strong feelings based on experience regarding what this role should and shouldn't be, and I discuss the rationale for my opinions in Chapter 1. I also believe CSOs must possess certain key traits to be successful, which are discussed in Chapter 2. As we get into this discussion on strategy, sometimes we find a negative connection around its success and usefulness. Consider the conclusions of a recent survey of 300 chief executive officers (CEOs). The key takeaway is that 72 percent of these CEOs believe that U.S. companies do a better job of developing corporate strategies than implementing them. The best military analogy I've heard that depicts this is: "The best strategy in the world can't take the hill." Translation: Strategy without execution is worthless. Creating a three-to-five-year strategy for a three-ring binder once a year that sits on your shelf is archaic. Creating a strategy that you in turn drive into actionable plans and goals with associated metrics is invaluable. Execution is everything. Great executors of business strategy create conditions where people:

- **Know what to do**—because accountabilities are clear.
- **Know how to do it**—because they have the right skills.
- **Are motivated to do it**—because they see how they are adding value to the organization.
- **Have defined metrics**—so they can consistently monitor and measure progress and results to make necessary course corrections and adjustments to achieve goals.

- **Have regular management forums**—so they can regularly vet problems, talk about changing competitive or market positions, or seek sage counsel from others on actions.

Now, in Part I, let's take a quick assessment of where we have come from, where we are at, and how to move forward and learn from Part II.

Chapter 1

Evolution of Strategic Planning and Today's Role: Chief Strategy Officer

Strategy without execution is a hallucination.
—Ambuj Goyal, General Manager, System
Storage and Networking, IBM

A primary role that has become more prominent in the last two to three years is the role of chief strategy officer (CSO). In the past, this role primarily fell on the leader of the business, the chief executive officer (CEO) or president. It also could fall on whichever senior business leader did corporate development (i.e., mergers and acquisitions), as likely that person was best suited to know the market and what other competitors had for value propositions that he or she might want to duplicate or embellish and to understand specific market forces. Today, with a globalized economy, the incredibly fast pace of change, and an insurmountable supply of information, business strategy is not something you can work on the side while doing another primary role. Or can you? This chapter goes through a very brief history of business strategy and quickly gets to today's CSO role and some perspective on what does and does not work in business strategy as we know it today.

Evolution of Strategic Planning

Strategic planning has certainly morphed over time. In contemplating this, think about decades of time versus years to look at trends and changes. One of the best articles I've read on this evolution was by Dr. Richard Oliver, who wrote "The Evolution of Business Strategy." I include some of the main excerpts and metaphors that he uses because they mirror my own philosophy of using ideas-that-stick metaphors. It's helpful to look through some of this history to try to predict what new megatrends and events will shape strategic planning and how we drive toward success.

Strategy as War. The word "strategy" is derived from the Greek word *strategia*, meaning "generalship." For early commercial enterprises that moved beyond the family firm, business approaches often mirrored those of the military. The command and control models Army generals used moved easily into business practice with little alteration. Company heads commanded the troops while winning battles through sheer force (superior resources), because they had an impenetrable fortress (a protected market or monopoly), or via guerrilla warfare (going after competitors when they're not expecting it). Some of these thematic elements still exist today. Many top executives regard Sun Tzu's *The Art of War*, written more than 2,000 years ago, as required reading. The command and control model has been pervasive. Strategy was primarily centered on winning the war by eliminating competitors.[1]

We know that a lot of how we organize and execute our businesses comes from the military. Think of the hierarchies and discipline utilized and required today. However, the days of one person being in charge and knowing all the factors and dealings in a business is gone. I'm not saying that there is not a head of a business— absolutely you need to have leader—but that person, today more than ever, needs to be a master orchestrator and organizer in pulling together the many aspects of a business in a globalized economy. While we still need to command and control, we need to do it in a more collaborative approach.

Strategy as Machine. World War II demonstrated that the winner was the one with the better "industrial machine." Thus, the war metaphor gave way to a view of strategy as essentially an industrial process that, just like a factory, was largely mechanized. The prescribed approaches to strategy seemed to suggest (just as with a machine), "If you press this button or pull this lever, then such and such will happen." With its new emphasis on mechanistic processes, the idea of strategic planning drew more attention in academic circles through the 1960s. Major corporations created strategic planning staffs and began to implement systematic planning processes. For the first time, strategy became a business process that was seen as manageable, in the same manner as other elements of the business. Many of today's key terms and tools—as well as a number of strategy consulting firms— were developed during this period. Courses on strategic planning began to enter the business school curriculum in a limited fashion.

Strategy as machine assumes a cookbook approach: "If you do 'x' then press 'y' button, then such and such will happen." This may have applied during a period of time, but obviously not today; life and business are just not that simple. Additionally, while there are some universal best practices on how to run a business, there is no singular, predefined path to success. There are too many other variables to consider, and after this part of time, post–World War II, the world has turned into an even smaller place. Information is readily available, the workforce no longer consists of the 30-year employees of the past, and older methods of success do not guarantee future success. If you depicted strategy as machine today, it would have to be a learning machine not unlike what you see in sci-fi movies that constantly adapt to their surroundings. Scary stuff.

Strategy as Network. The global shocks of the 1970s (escalating oil prices, war, government instability, and increasing global competition) illustrated the importance of flexibility, non-linear thinking (i.e., strategy was not simply an extension of current trends), and rapid communication in strategic thinking. Many companies burdened with a rigid planning process—or no planning process at all—suffered devastating consequences.

The 1980s saw the rise of Japan and its consequent effect on strategic planning theory and practice. The rapid advances in technology also had a dramatic effect, with the humble bar code turning inventory management upside down and the rise of enterprise resource planning (ERP) computer systems allowing managers to track widespread geographic activity in real time. Harvard professor and strategy guru Michael Porter wrote his most important works during this period and shaped several generations of academic and practitioner thinking about strategy. As the personal computer and advanced robotics became more widespread, productivity increased and managers gained a wider view of operations than ever before. The 1980s were a golden time in the history of strategy: The decade witnessed the start of global planning processes and corporate reengineering.

The 1990s were a boom time for the United States, which sealed its role as the dominant world leader. Strategic thinking was affected by the rise of the Internet, accelerating advances in technology of all kinds, and a striving for efficiency and low-cost production, putting the focus on a firm's ability to "add and migrate value." Strategic planning and continual revision became entrenched as a vital core of the corporation.

Strategy as network was important. It caused a realization that you could not be so inwardly focused on your own products and business as to ignore the market, your customers, and your competitors. However, as the 1990s led to strategic planning becoming entrenched as a vital core of the corporation, it also led to some of today's naysayers considering "strategy" a bad thing. As with anything good, strategy needs to be in balance and not overdone. Taking a good thing too far, swinging the pendulum too far to one side or another, can turn a strength into a weakness. Those corporations that put in large strategic planning departments and got buried in the administration of creating lengthy, inflexible plans drove leadership and strategy to a place of bureaucracy and low value added for the time invested. But at the same time, as noted, some of the best strategic planning models, like Michael Porter's work, came into play and are still very pertinent today.

Strategy as Biology. Perhaps the most important change in strategic thinking in this period was the recognition of the critical role customers played and their intimate relationship with the "ecology" of the firm. With few exceptions (e.g., government-dictated monopolies) the customer has always been the final arbitrator of corporate strategic success, particularly over the long term. However, as a result of the proliferation of information technologies during the late 1990s, the customer role in strategy formulation became more immediate and instantly powerful, influencing the life of the firm just as a living organism interacts with its environment. This strong and continuous interaction of a firm with its environment (particularly its customers) begged for a new metaphor, that of an organism.

Interesting, isn't it? Takes you right back to biology 101 and the study of amoebas. Why did it take so long to come around to the notion of providing customers what they want, and you'll in turn have a successful business? While the Internet changed distribution channels for selling products forever, before that, the Internet simply changed who had what information. Now customers of products and services had a wealth of knowledge and information at their fingertips via the Internet, and they were not blindly buying based on marketing alone. Think of blogs, consumer reviews, star ratings on Amazon.com, and the many other customer feedback points on goods and services. Customers have the knowledge today, and they have a large voice in the market and can affect it very, very quickly.

Strategy Today. What is strategy today if innovation and change are being created as a natural and intimate part of a constantly mutating organism? Strategy is the process of understanding the industry (its ecology) and the firm's position in that industry (its genetic makeup). It involves understanding whether the firm can either improve the structure of its industry or improve its position within the industry (either a revolutionary or evolutionary path.) It asks the question: Can the firm be better than average in its current industry (get beyond its DNA)? If not, it must change the structure of the industry or place itself in another industry where it can be dominant and or relevant (mutate or die).

If you believe the premise that, today, a business and its strategy are part of a constantly mutating organism, then I think you have the mind-set needed to succeed in business at this point in history. Information is fluid, markets are global, customer knowledge and feedback are instant, financial market evaluations are quick and come with high expectations. If you are not constantly adapting, you are dying. Makes you want to run out and start a business, doesn't it? It's really not that bad, but you do need to have your head on a swivel and be aware of your environment. Today's world requires collaboration, teamwork, and trust among the team to move swiftly. It also calls for empowerment and delegation. It is very difficult to run a business in today's world, out of the proverbial corner office, as one person making all the decisions. The world has simply become a more complex, nimble, demanding place. Those who are adapting to today's new rules of engagement are thriving; others are falling to the wayside.

New Role: Chief Strategy Officer

In today's mutating environment, what type of changes should your business be considering? New roles pop up in corporations from time to time to address new or emerging trends in the marketplace. While there have long been people responsible for strategy, only recently have we had a dedicated C-suite position responsible for this role in some larger companies. I've seen this named position pop up more and more. There are pure CSO roles, and then there are hybrid CSO roles. The hybrid roles usually have another function responsibility, such as:

- Chief strategy and innovation officer
- Chief strategy and product development officer
- Chief strategy and corporate development officer
- Chief strategy and marketing officer

First, let's look at the core of a pure CSO role, and then we weigh the pros and cons of the hybrid roles.

Strategy Starts at the Top

It only makes sense that the CEO/president has someone on staff responsible for "facilitating" strategy. I specifically use the term "facilitating" strategy rather than "responsibility for" strategy because there is a huge difference. When you put one person in charge of or make him or her solely responsible for strategy, then you could have a scapegoat who is responsible for all future successes or failures of the company. There is no "I" in team, right? Well, there is no "I" in strategy either. The desired goal is an entire executive team that is creating, developing, testing, and executing on business strategy. It may be one person's full-time job to facilitate that work, but that person is not solely responsible for it. If one person does all the strategic thinking and planning, that person becomes a crutch to the organization and strategies can be one dimensional. The other executives can get caught up in the day-to-day details of running the business and not also have a watchful eye on opportunities, risks, trends, and other strategic areas that the whole executive team should be paying attention to.

Why Can't This Role Simply Remain with the CEO/President?

Why do you need a CSO? Simply put, CEOs need help; they can't be everywhere at once. As a matter of fact, the best CEO–CSO relationships I've seen are where the CEO is so comfortable in the role (and his or her own skin) that he or she consistently seeks the advice and feedback of others on issues. And if the CEO has a CSO on staff, this person is the CEO's consigliere on decisions and strategic thinking. Not that the two should always think alike; if they always did, one of them would not be required. But when you have a ying to your yang and someone you can speak extraneously with and bat strategic ideas around in a safe zone, that is an effective relationship, one where business strategy can be incubated then further developed with others. Today's CEO needs to deal with matrixed organization structures, globalization, new laws and regulations, shorter product life cycles, demanding cost reductions, and an insatiable appetite by markets, customers, and investors for innovations. Therefore, the role of the CSO has emerged—not to replace or remove the CEO from doing business strategy, but to help that executive and facilitate the larger executive team.

Is Business Strategy Work a Full-Time Job? Isn't Business Strategy Work a Once-a-Year Job?

Good questions, and ones to which I have very specific answers. I'd answer those questions with "Yes and no, it depends." Let me explain.

Second Question First I don't believe business strategy is an annual, once-per-year-only process any longer. You simply can't afford to ignore markets, competitors, trends, clients, government, technology, and economics for nine months out of the year, after you put together a plan. You have to monitor changes and trends constantly.

Not to say you shouldn't create a plan and execute it, because if you wait for perfect and complete information, you will never move forward. But a business strategy evolves; it cannot stay stagnant for a year. You learn new things, factors changes, the market has turbulence, customers give you feedback, and then you may tweak or outright change parts of your strategy. So I do not believe this is a once-a-year process, but it also is not a process where you should be tweaking PowerPoint slides to improve your story. Who cares about the slides?! Really! And this from a guy who has made a living on creating them! Yes, the slides are important to tell your story convincingly to stakeholders, but it's the content and the strategic thinking within that matter, not the PowerPoint gimmicks. Spend your time in strategic thinking, not color palette controversies.

Back to the First Question Is business strategy work a full-time job? My response: "Yes, absolutely, *but* with a qualification." The qualification is that I don't believe the CSO role should always be a "pure" strategy role. I believe many times the CSO also needs to be responsible for another operational area of the business, such as product, marketing, operations, customer experience, and so on. If the CSO is a pure position, the person can get caught in the ivory tower pontificating strategy and quickly get out of touch with the operations of the business. If the CSO owns a part of the business, the person has vested skin in the game as an operator and is respected by peers. I firmly believe this hybrid role is more effective in almost all situations. So the CSO should have the following "CSO traits" and responsibilities plus another logical functional/operational area that makes sense in that business and likely is tangential to the CSO role anyway:

- **Master of multitasking.** One study revealed that CSOs are responsible for an average of 10 major business functions and activities, as diverse and demanding as mergers and acquisitions, competitive analysis and market research, and long-range planning. They must be capable of quickly switching between environments and activities.

- **Jack-of-all-trades.** Most strategy executives reported that they had significant line management and functional experience in such areas as technology management, marketing, and operations. Less than one-fifth had spent the bulk of their pre-CSO careers on strategic planning.

- **Star player.** Most CSOs achieved impressive business results earlier in their careers and view the strategy role as a launching pad, not a landing pad.

- **Doer, not just thinker.** Although CSOs split their time almost evenly between strategy development and execution, their bias must be toward the latter.

- **Good handle on short- and long-term issues.** The medium term—that period from one to four years out—can go unattended, however. CSOs must focus the organization's attention here, the critical period for strategy execution.
- **Influencer, not a dictator.** Strategy chiefs don't succeed by pulling rank. They sway others with their deep industry knowledge, their organizational connections, and their ability to communicate effectively, not using the cover of "Your CEO wants you to do this."
- **Comfortable with ambiguity.** All executives today must exhibit this trait, but it's especially true for CSOs, whose actions typically won't pay off for years. The role tends to evolve rapidly and requires an extraordinary ability to embrace an uncertain future.
- **Objectivity.** Given their broad role, CSOs can't play favorites. Openly partisan CSOs, or those who let emotions or the strength of other personalities cloud their vision, are sure to fail.

More and more companies are exploring the CSO option. For those striving for high performance, adding a seasoned, energetic CSO is often similar to a professional sports organization signing a top veteran player from another team. It simply improves the chances of beating the opposition. To fulfill this quest, CEOs are either tapping internal company veterans with the experience and the social and political capital to cross boundaries quickly and effectively, or they're bringing outsiders and their fresh growth perspectives into the C-suite. Either way, they're recognizing the ever-growing value of having a trusted, in-house strategy expert as a member of the top team, an executive who will keep the company focused through both the formulation and the execution of its strategy.

What Type of Chief Strategy Officer Is Needed?

I don't have a one-size-fits-all answer to this question, but we'll explore core components. I came across an interesting discussion on a blog about what is needed in a CSO. Here are some of the responses:

- Big question! I really believe a CSO needs to be a career practitioner (versus manager/administrator). Beyond that, my response is "exactly whatever the business needs."
- Ability to view the entire business holistically and micro-view critical areas and make or recommend decisions based on strategic benefit to the organization. Be a great listener and team leader.
- This person should also be able to implement. Strategy without implementation is nothing.

- Good CSOs have to have command of many basic business skills. They need to understand finance, competition, sales, and, to an extent, the technical side. In my experience, great CSOs come with a wide range of experiences. They also need to be highly creative and willing to wield influence. Most CSO positions are in advisory roles to the profit and loss leaders. Therefore, they have to be great communicators and facilitators.

    In addition, the CSO should be able to deploy these skills in answering the following questions effectively: how to grow, how to compete, and how to remain efficient.

- The CSO has to play a big role in setting the corporate strategic directions of the business, identifying the strategic initiatives that bring high value to the business, developing and maintaining short and long business plans, and monitoring strategy implementation, and they must be able to advise on strategic tactics in highly increasing competition environment.

- If we see strategy as how to realize the vision of the CEO/board, then some of the skills set of the CSO are: externalizing the tacit concerns of the CEO/board, supporting them in actually understanding how these concerns have an impact on the vision, ensuring relevant risks and complexities are identified from various levels within the organization, ensuring the current internal capacity to deliver is taken into account, keeping abreast with external developments, ensuring there is alignment between the various levels of decision making, including feedback loops, and ensuring emerging concerns are managed appropriately.

- Oftentimes strategy is defined during implementation. You must be able to recognize what is successful and what isn't. Strategy is not developing an idea or plan and passing it off to the next team to implement.

These bloggers collectively get it. Being an effective CSO and driving and facilitating strategy is about relationships, consistency, execution, and linkage to mission.

Let's look at actual deliverables, and ask, what does a CSO do? Consider this real, slightly redacted job description from a 2013 posting for a chief strategy and innovation officer position:

Position Overview

In support of its ambitious business and social impact goals, <ACME COMPANY> is currently seeking a seasoned executive to spearhead an integrated set of functions: ongoing strategic planning and innovation, strategic relationship management, organizational effectiveness, and corporate brand management. This hire will join a highly collaborative seven-member executive team and play a major role in increasing the organization's overall capacity and potential for impact. This is an exciting opportunity for a thoughtful and resourceful senior leader and manager to help advance <ACME'S> double bottom line of maintaining the organization's business strength while creating unprecedented change on the people and communities it serves.

CS&I Officer—Responsibilities:

1. Strategic Thinking and Planning (30%)
   - In collaboration with the executive team, lead the ongoing and active strategic thinking process, translating the two-year strategic plan into specific implementation strategies that position <ACME> as a transformative leader in the field.
   - Oversee the management of corporate-level process on an ongoing basis, advising business units in strategic execution. Continue to improve processes that are both top-down and bottom-up, and

(*Continued*)

(Continued)

include <ACME>'s Board of Directors where appropriate.

2. Innovation (20%)
   - Ensure an innovation discipline that identifies and incubates ideas to create scalable solutions that lead to growth in the organization's double bottom line of creating business value and social impact.
   - Oversee ongoing innovation processes and related innovation labs to ensure the ongoing development of new markets, partnerships, and products in the organization's core sectors.

3. Strategic Relationship Development and Management (20%)
   - Develop high-level relationships with prospective and existing funders, managing <ACME>'s brand and brand messaging to foundations, and identifying new opportunities for philanthropic support.
   - Champion and refine as needed the existing strategy and approach for pursuing philanthropic opportunities, including overseeing

processes for customer relationship management and proposal creation.

4. Social Impact Assessment (10%)
   - Directly manage <ACME's> further development of its approach to assess the social impact of its business activities, and continue to move the process from assessing outputs to outcomes.
   - Ensure that this process is based on the ongoing need for clear and evident organizational learning, such that understanding of our impact leads to greater capacity to set business objectives that lead to increasingly higher impact outcomes.

5. Staff Management and Organizational Effectiveness (10%)
   - Take responsibility for and refine strategies pertaining to human capital management and organizational effectiveness such as team development, performance management, change management, and organizational culture. Stay abreast of related theory and changing practices.

(Continued)

(Continued)

- Supervise a team currently comprised of a Director of Innovation and Director of Social Impact. Determine other staffing needs and grow team as needed.

6. Corporate Communications and Brand Management (<10%)

- Lead the Executive Team in an analysis of the existing corporate communications, brand management, social media programs and staffing needs relative to that function in the future.

Desired Skills and Experience

Qualifications:

- 10+ years of executive experience in community development lending or similar field such as financial services, management consulting, or real estate development
- A demonstrated commitment to the mission of <ACME>, with a belief and interest in achieving transformative social objectives through business acumen and techniques

- Consummate strategic leadership and management skills, including competence in decision making, change management, staff management, and organizational effectiveness
- Demonstrated experience leading innovation efforts for an organization, with a track record of balancing risk and pragmatism, and tying ideation to business objectives
- A skilled relationship builder and communicator, with a natural ability to serve both internal and external customers
- Collaborative and comfort being part of a consensus-driven leadership team
- An ability to embrace and model <ACME>'s core values of cooperation, innovation, leadership, commitment, trust, and diversity
- Content experience in community development, lending, finance, and/or practice areas of <ACME> (health care, affordable housing, education, healthy foods, aging) is strongly desired
- Master's Degree in business, finance, or related field is strongly preferred

What are the four key takeaways from reading this job description and description of the candidate?

1. **A seasoned and strategic player.** If there is an internal candidate who knows the operations well, he or she may be a good candidate, especially if there has already been a lot of churn on the executive team. If the team has a lot of tenure, it may be time to bring someone in who can bring additional diversity to it. Either way, a respected, seasoned person in business strategy is required.

2. **A relationship builder and doer.** It's all about relationships, right? Why else would many of us jump on a plane to go see a client when we could have simply made a phone call or have written an e-mail? Because you are building a relationship. This stuff is important and you are a doer. Everyone respects a doer, someone who gets stuff done, doesn't just talk, and isn't in the same place the next time you find them, still talking.

3. **Multiple areas of adjacent responsibilities.** In this case, this role has responsibility for corporate communications, innovation, brand management, and fundraising. Smart. Give the person the role of master facilitator but also give him or her some operations to own and have a test lab in.

4. **Collaborator and facilitator.** Last, it's key that the role will, in collaboration with the executive

team, lead the strategic thinking process. Don't make this person solely responsible for the thinking or the strategies. He or she should be the facilitator, the collaborator of strategy.

Of course, every role is going to be different depending on the company, the business model maturity, the tenets of the organization, the existing executive team, the CEO—a whole host of factors. But my core philosophy holds true in all of them: Name a CSO-plus position on the executive team reporting to the CEO. Have that person responsible for facilitating and consulting on business strategy with the CEO and the entire business. In addition to this core responsibility, have the CSO be the head of a functional area(s) that makes sense in your business and on your team, such as product development, marketing, innovation, or customer experience.

CSO: A Distributed Solution versus a Singular Role

I gave a lot of detail regarding what a CSO position could look like via the full job description you just read. I did this to show one good example of how complex and multifaceted a position this can be. I also gave some blogger opinions on what they thought a CSO should be to highlight the fact that there is no shortage of opinions on the topic, but most agree that it is a large and complex role. As a leader, when you look at a role like this and understand its complexity, you should begin to ask yourself whether one person really can do this or whether the job should be the responsibility of several individuals. CEOs fight with these questions all the time. In large organizations, everyone wants to be at the CEO's direct staff table to represent their areas, but a CEO can't have 50 direct reports. The opposite is true in smaller companies: Individuals are forced to wear many hats, must execute on many duties, and must divide up these responsibilities. Small companies can't afford to have full-time CSOs. So what is the right answer? Again, it depends (of course). I'd argue that without one person responsible for facilitating this work, then no one is responsible. It's next to impossible to manage by committee; someone has to be the one throat to choke. However, if you have a fully functional and capable executive team in place with no gaps, it may make sense to distribute this role across a couple key leaders. In this case, the division of responsibilities and having clear roles is critical.

Summary

Conclusion. There is a clear one-two punch to get respect in business strategy—develop relationships and then execute. It's hard to argue with a successful track record, especially one in which it was a relay race and multiple people contributed to the win.

Gold nuggets you took away to share with your board of directors or your staff, or for personal reflection:

1. _____

2. _____

Three Additional Resources/Tools

The Art of War **by Sun Tzu.** If you want to read a book that hasn't gotten much publicity in recent years but is a core book in business strategy (assuming you subscribe to the fact that military strategy is similar to business strategy), this is the book to read.

Careerbuilder.com. Go online and look at CSO job descriptions like the one shown in this chapter. Use this and other job descriptions as a guide to determine what responsibilities you think you should have in this role in your company based on your specific needs.

Your company's executive team organization chart. Look at the chart and map who is doing the CSO's role and if it is being covered adequately or if you have a gap. This should be a very interesting exercise.

Note

1. All quotations are from Richard Oliver, "The Evolution of Business Strategy," *Journal of Business Strategy* (September–October 2001).

Chapter 2

Emotional Intelligence: Being "Facilitative and Consultative"

Coming together is a beginning; keeping together is progress; working together is success.

—Henry Ford

Every businessperson knows a story about a highly intelligent, highly skilled executive who was promoted into a leadership position only to fail at the job. And every businessperson also knows a story about someone with solid—but not extraordinary—intellectual abilities and technical skills who was promoted into a similar position and then soared.

Such anecdotes support the widespread belief that identifying individuals with the "right stuff" to be leaders is more art than science. After all, the personal styles of superb leaders vary: Some leaders are subdued and analytical; others shout their manifestos from the mountaintops. And just as important, different situations call for different types of leadership. Most mergers need a sensitive negotiator at the helm; whereas many turnarounds require a more forceful authority.

I believe that the most effective leaders are alike in one crucial way: They all have a high degree of what has come to be known as emotional intelligence (EQ). It's not that intellectual intelligence (IQ) and technical skills are irrelevant. IQ does matter, but mainly as a threshold capability; that is, IQ is the entry-level requirement for executive positions. But, without EQ, a person can have the best training in the world, an insightful, analytical mind, and an endless supply of smart ideas, but he or she still won't make a great leader. Consider reading the book *Geeks and Geezers*.[1] It is a great study on what makes a good leader, looking at both young and more seasoned leaders. Although the authors don't specifically discuss EQ, they refer to "crucibles"—moments that everyone at one point or another went through that shaped who they are and what their company would become. I categorize crucibles into experiential executive shaping and part of the EQ equation. How is EQ related to the specific behaviors we associate with leadership effectiveness? Several studies have shown that higher levels of EQ are associated with better performance in these areas:

- Participative management
- Putting people at ease
- Self-awareness
- Balance between personal life and work
- Straightforwardness and composure
- Building and mending relationships
- Doing whatever it takes
- Decisiveness
- Confronting problem employees
- Change management

Countless studies and articles have been written about what makes for good leadership and leaders. One component of this discussion is around leadership style, business background, intellect, and these factors exhibited in a model of art versus science. Which is the more important aspect of leadership and business strategy and execution, art or science? I believe that equal parts of both are necessary. I know, that sounds like an easy way out, but it's true. Think ying and yang. You need a balance of both to lead, execute, and be successful:

- **Science.** You need to have baseline skills and solid management principles just to get to the party. You need to have an arsenal of models, techniques, common vernacular, and some history of lessons learned in your business or market as well as other skills. What is the saying, "Those who don't learn from history are doomed to repeat it"? Yep, I'll

buy that. You cannot ignore some certain universal truths in business, similar to nonnegotiables in
science, like gravity. You need to have the "science"
background, education, and experience to be successful. Else you could get your picture in the *Wall
Street Journal* for something very naive.

- **Art.** You have the science, the knowledge, skills, and
  historical references to be successful. Do you really
  need anything else? Getting by with just the science
  and not the art component is like skating through
  life just on your good looks alone. Sooner or later,
  it will bite you, and it won't last forever. I'd also
  suggest that those people who are good with the
  art component, perhaps even stronger in it than in
  the science, are the better leaders and have greater
  success. It is less about them and more about the
  team. It is less about facts and ego and more about
  customers and experience. But, again, you swing
  this pendulum too far, and you are a touchy-feely
  business that bends over unnecessarily, doesn't make
  a profit, and is soon not a going concern. The art of
  business and strategy centers on being able to facilitate through strategy and change effectively, making judgment calls, anticipating competitive moves,
  predicting the market and changes, and motivating
  people. These are not lessons learned from books so
  much as they are inherent and learned over time by
  individuals.

Characterizations

In the past, I have told various staff members to "be consultative and facilitative." If you ever interview with me, I'll ask you this for certain: "Give me an example of how you have been consultative and facilitative in your last role, and tell me how you think you will be in this new role." I want to know how people problem-solve, how they help others to problem-solve, and how they facilitate and lead to solutions. Often I remind staff: "You don't need to have all the answers. You just have to be able to ask the right questions." That is why I think an individual who has solid business strategy skills can succeed in any industry. Same process, different products and markets. The University of St. Thomas Executive MBA program in Minneapolis, Minnesota, subscribes to this thinking. Its goal is not to teach to facts and answers to a business or function but rather to general management skills so you can thrive and lead in any function of any organization in any situation. It's about having a general manager's holistic mind-set and thinking systemically. Let's further this discussion by applying some definitions for later context.

Emotional Intelligence. Emotional intelligence (EQ) refers to the ability to perceive, control, and evaluate emotions. Some researchers suggest that emotional intelligence can be

learned and strengthened, while others claim it
is an inborn characteristic.[2]

The earliest roots of EQ can be traced to Charles
Darwin's work on the importance of emotional expression for survival and adaptation. In the 1900s, even
though traditional definitions of intelligence were
around cognitive aspects such as memory and problem
solving, several influential researchers in the intelligence
field of study had begun to recognize the importance
of the noncognitive aspects.

It was Daniel Goleman[3] who first brought the term
"emotional intelligence" to a wide audience with his
1995 book of that name, and it was Goleman who first
applied the concept to business with his 1998 *Harvard
Business Review* article. In his research at nearly 200
large, global companies, Goleman found that while the
qualities traditionally associated with leadership—such
as intelligence, toughness, determination, and vision—
are required for success, they are insufficient. Truly
effective leaders are also distinguished by a high degree
of EQ, which includes self-awareness, self-regulation,
social skill, empathy, and motivation.

- **Self-awareness.** The ability to know one's
  emotions, strengths, weaknesses, drives, values,
  and goals and recognize their impact on others while using gut feelings to guide decisions.

- **Self-regulation.** Involves controlling or redirecting one's disruptive emotions and impulses and adapting to changing circumstances.
- **Social skill.** Managing relationships to move people in the desired direction.
- **Empathy.** Considering other people's feelings, especially when making decisions.
- **Motivation.** Being driven to achieve for the sake of achievement.

Consultative A consultant (from the Latin *consultare* means "to discuss"; we also derive words such as *consul* and *counsel* from this word) is a professional who provides advice in a particular area of expertise. To me, good consultants truly are "consultative": They offer multiple, properly timed suggestions, not singular solutions and one-time answers with no rationale to the thinking behind the solutions. I call this cook-book consulting—have a problem, prescribe a solution, done. To be consultative, they need to encourage leap-frog thinking (people building on each other's ideas back and forth to create a synergistic solution) and dialog that builds with a group, not just individuals speaking or waiting for their turn to speak. They offer suggestions from other industries' experiences, push limits and boundaries, go past what their client is comfortable with discussing. They know how to facilitate through and get maximum output from divergent, then convergent thinking and discussion of ideas. They know how to artfully give people line to run and explore an idea or strategy but also know when and how to reel them in when needed and refocus a group. This is where I distinguish being a "consultant" and being "consultative." The science piece that consultants normally bring to the table focuses on methodologies and frameworks that they utilize to structure conversation, identify problems, and frame solutions and scenarios. Being consultative is the art piece that distinguishes the good consultant from the great consultant.

Facilitative You are the master of ceremonies. You control the process, the room, and the outcomes. You get everyone to participate fairly. You gently hold back the extreme extroverts—you pull them to the side if you need to on a break so they are not disruptive or squelching others. You call on the introverts to participate and get their voices heard. You adapt your style and time frame to that of the group but don't get bulldozed by the group. You are the facilitator.

When I named my business Mercury Business Advisors, I had in mind the idea of being facilitative, consultative, and aiding others in defining and executing strategy. On my Website, I describe my personal belief that there is no one, universal elixir or secret sauce that makes a business succeed but a combination of factors that makes a business successful. In describing the genesis of my business name, I wrote:

> Alchemists from the early Renaissance period searched for a secret elixir that would turn other elements into gold. At one point, they thought that element was Mercury, but it was not, and the search continued.
>
> Similarly in business today, leaders are looking for that secret elixir or "secret sauce" to grow, innovate, execute, and improve their businesses, but there is no ONE secret sauce. Success in business depends on your strategy, business model, competition, market turbulence, product portfolio and evolution, etc, and there are a series of decisions to be made and execution that needs to occur. Mercury Business Advisors is here to help facilitate making and executing on those choices. To facilitate and consult with you on how to find the secret sauce that your business may be missing.[4]

I share this here because I think it is important. The best consulting houses and advisory firms are not about singular solutions and telling you answers; they are about listening and facilitating you through a realization of what is needed in your business and being consultative along the way. I think this is the epitome of the old phrase "Give a man a fish, and you have fed him once. Teach him how to fish, and you have fed him for a lifetime." Hiring consultants who don't ever end their scope of work is not healthy or helpful in the long run. Think about some of the best consultants and consulting houses you've used in the past: Do they drive you to a singular solution, or do they consult and facilitate more holistically?

Innovation and Linkage to Business Strategy

As we discuss being consultative and facilitative and explore art versus science, my mind keeps going to a discussion on innovation. Innovation within a company is a perfect example of how a leader needs to be consultative and facilitative in approach and how he or she also needs to apply science and art to be successful. Every company and leader wants to be seen as innovative; customers and financial markets clamor for innovation. Why don't we do a better job of innovation? How do we better get innovation into the business and not just as a one-time event? Let's take a deeper look at innovation and its link to business strategy.

Being consultative and facilitative applies to innovation the same as it does to business strategy. Innovation should not be done solely for innovation's sake (e.g., I'm innovating because it's in vogue). Innovation should be done with the clear purpose of driving and advancing business strategy. Great companies in existence today drive and support innovation, but I think they fall into two camps. I'm not an insider at either company; this is my external perspective from having watched them and talked with some of their leaders. First is the Google camp. No disrespect to Google. It is a very successful company, and its owners are not intent on the status quo and want to push the envelope. In that vein, Google has a robust innovation area that works on very far-reaching ideas and products that are totally unrelated to the company's core business. This can be noble and beneficial to the community and can create some totally new businesses, but is that the mission of Google? What about the theory of leveraging core competencies and divesting anything that is not core to your business or doesn't support your mission? I believe this innovation at Google is good, but perhaps it would be more appropriate for a think-tank company to incubate these innovations and for Google to divest or sell these product ideas rather than divert core resources and assets from its main business.

The second innovation camp is the 3M model. 3M, the home of the sticky note. If you have read anything on innovation and know anything about 3M, you know the company is the poster child of innovation. In the past, the company has promoted "Innovation Fridays," where employees spend a portion of their time each week postulating new products and markets—ideas that are supportive of the 3M core mission and utilize its core capabilities. 3M measures innovation (not an easy task) by reporting new product introductions and revenue from those new products over the last three years. This shows the health of the business and if it is stagnant or innovating. I like the idea of the Google camp of innovation and find it sexy and exciting, but I believe the 3M camp of innovation is a more appropriate innovation method for companies to help achieve and drive their core business strategies and consistently drive more shareholder value.

How do you drive and promote innovation across the business? If you are leading innovation efforts, you need to serve in a couple of roles. You are the facilitator of getting innovation to occur. That doesn't mean that you come up with all the ideas; it means you put vehicles, processes, and channels in place to capture, explore, evaluate, and rapidly test and deploy new innovative concepts and products. Innovation is not a department or one rainmaker with ideas or a flavor-of-the-month program; it should be a value that is promoted and driven through the business. In the past, I've created multiple innovation channels to drive innovation throughout businesses by having:

- **Open submission channels.** These channels are for all employees. Think of them as electronic suggestion boxes for idea capture. Yes, you can argue that many ideas that come in via these channels have already been tried, are not fully thought out, or can be downright silly or bad for the business. However, for that one good idea that comes along out of ten not-so-good ones, it's worth it. Also, think about your employees. Employees want a way in which they can be heard. This type of program provides that avenue. These ideas can also be further delineated between product ideas and process improvement ideas. Then, when you are taking in these ideas, you can forward the product ones to product development and the process ones to your quality group for review.
- **Monthly business challenges.** In setting up monthly challenges, you are asking your employee base for solutions to specific business problems. Rather than an open submission of ideas, as in the last item, with these challenges you are telling employees, "Hey, you guys all have unique perspectives and ideas. How would you solve this particular business problem?" I've found this channel to be much more successful than open submission. Open submission takes some creativity in coming up with the original idea and doesn't give much of a framework for idea development. In this challenge

channel, you give the original idea of the problem with some context, and employees have to solve it. Many people are good problem solvers. Given the right parameters, they can offer many good, creative solutions. Just structure a business challenge, but allow enough blank space for freedom of response, and ask your employees!

- **Fellowship channels.** I had a PDE (proudly discovered elsewhere) moment when I saw this channel from another division of a company I worked at. I like PDE moments because they are an admission that there are lots of innovative ideas, products, concepts, and the like that have been created but not applied or executed in other industries or companies. Hence the name PDE, and the innovation is executing that idea in YOUR environment. The channel I refer to offered a sabbatical or fellowship opportunity to one individual per year to purpose a "big idea" for the business. I morphed the idea a bit, but the concept was simple. Present this challenge:

  - Do you have a big idea for the business? Do you have a little entrepreneurial itch but want a safe environment and resources at your disposal? Does your boss not listen to your idea, or is he or she not convinced? Do you want some time to explore and run with this idea? Well, then today is your lucky day! You may be eligible to be selected to work on your project for the next six months, either full or part time. Your current job responsibilities would be covered by someone else, and you'd return to your job after your fellowship is complete (unless you are so successful that you create a new position for yourself based on the fellowship work). You will get assigned a coach, a mentor to help you navigate the organization to get the resources you need. Your mentor will be a sounding board to you as you struggle through execution. Your mentor should motivate you.

For a hungry, talented type-A person, this sounds like a dream. I think this is a smart program and approach to get some big ideas on the table that create some excitement in the organization that drives employee morale, and, in the end, innovates to drive business effectiveness and efficiency. If you do this right, you will create some intense competition of projects and high employee satisfaction—and what chief executive officer (CEO) doesn't want that?

- **Future-sensing groups**. I used this channel in the past to both generate and test ideas. Earlier renditions were more pure think tanks, heavy on IQ, but as I learned and shared, later these teams I created were more holistic and had strong EQs as well—they were about smart ideas, relationships, and execution. Typically I would say to my peers on the executive team or the CEO, "Give me one or two nominees from each function that you see as a thought leader, innovator, can-do resource, energetic, and deserving to sit with similar peers to come up with and test ideas in our business."

Many were considered. Who wouldn't want to be associated with a think tank group and gain some recognition from executives like that? So it was pretty easy to pull candidates together for the group. But rather than just creating ideas, I found that using the future sensing group to test other ideas and strategies was also very effective. I would use this group as a feeder to the business strategy planning process. Let employees come up with a solid SWOT (strengths, weaknesses, opportunities, and threats) analysis and then let the executive team tear it up. This type of model really gives leadership teams a great indication of what is on the minds of the best and brightest folks in the business.

Another responsibility to drive innovation through the business to achieve business strategy is to be a nag. Yup, be a nag. I say this because that is what some functional leaders would call it. In the world of quality, one of the simplest yet most effective tools is the Five Whys. The Five Whys is simple: When you are vetting a business issue or reviewing a business strategy, ask "Why?" five times. When you keep challenging and asking why, you are peeling back the onion and understanding the core reasoning and value in doing something. If the whys are answered quickly and thoughtfully, the strategy is usually sound and well thought out. When leaders struggle with the why questions and get defensive, or give the parental "because-I-said" response, that is when you know you hit a nerve and a potential issue. It is our job as leaders to question, challenge, improve, and drive. But if you challenge and ask questions that appear to doubt someone's intellect and decision making, you better pack a lunch because it's going to be a fight, and not a fun one. However, if you ask the whys in an emotionally sensitive and thoughtful way, leaders are much more apt to respond in a noncombative way. Then they consider the advice and questions as stimulating their strategy and as helpful to the cause, not condemning and intrusive.

How does this role sound? Piece of cake, right? Not really. But when you have a CEO who supports the CSO and a leadership team that understands the CSO role as a facilitator and internal consultant for their use, not someone or a function that is auditing them, you'll have a powerful force. Additionally, the person in the CSO role needs to be confident but humble and a bit self-deprecating. If the CSO does not exhibit confidence, who is going to listen to him or her? But if the

CSO is a windbag, doesn't care to listen, and prefers to talk and preach to others, how long do you think other leaders are going to follow him or her?

Summary

Conclusion. Many leaders have the IQ necessary to run a business. However, the best leaders (CEOs, CSOs, etc.) have high EQs and are tuned in to how others react and interact with them, employees, customers, and other stakeholders. IQ is table stakes; EQ is needed to achieve greatness.

Gold nuggets you took away to share with your board of directors or your staff, or for personal reflection:

1. _____

2. _____

Additional Resources/Tools

More on EQ. Read any of Daniel Goleman's books on EQ: *Emotional Intelligence*; *The Power of Emotional Intelligence*; *Working with Emotional Intelligence*. Consider the leadership shadow you cast and the soft skills required to be a great facilitator and leader.

More on innovation. Read anything from Clayton Christenson, but start with *The Innovator's Dilemma*, a bible in the world of innovation.

Read *Speed of Trust* by Stephen M. R. Covey and Rebecca R. Merrill. Premise: When you have high trust with someone or a team of people, how much faster do you move on getting things done? When you have trust, things fly.

Notes

1. Warren G. Bennis and Robert J. Thomas, *Geeks and Geezers* (Boston, MA: Harvard Business Review Press, 2002).

2. http://psychology.about.com/library/quiz/bl_eq_quiz.htm.

3. Daniel Goleman, *Emotional Intelligence: Why It Can Matter More than IQ* (New York: Bantam, 1995).

4. Mercury Business Advisors Inc. http://www.mercuryba .com/index.html.

Part II

PARABLES
THAT TEACH
AND PORTRAY
BUSINESS
STRATEGY

I am guessing most readers have heard of the essay "All I Really Need to Know I Learned in Kinder-garten" by Robert Fulghum. If not, look it up for a good read or refresher; it's worth it. In the end, it's about simple, straightforward concepts like sharing, taking re-sponsibility, playing fair, cleaning up your own mess, taking an occasional nap, and having balance in life.

These are all things that worked in kindergarten and should be paid more attention to in adolescent and adult life. But, somewhere along the line, and its different timing for everyone, life starts to get complicated. It gets intense, confusing, and overly complex. Then, many times, some life event happens, and we need to get grounded and go back to the basics. In this part of the book, I apply Fulghum's concept to highlight lessons learned in business strategy. I hope this fun yet basic framework resonates (and entertains a bit), provides you with some gold nugget ideas or reminders, and helps you get back to the basics that you may have forgotten or not paid enough attention to lately. You may not relate to all of the five chapters in this part, but that is okay; find the one(s) you most relate to and file those stories in your head for later reference. For a little fun, here are titles of chapters that didn't make it past the editor:

- *Everything I Needed to Learn about Business Strategy I Learned* (EINTLABSIL) . . . from My Dog
- EINTLABSIL . . . from the Bottom of a Bottle of Stoli's Vodka
- EINTLABSIL . . . from the Suck-up in the Front Row of My MBA Class
- EINTLABSIL . . . from Two of My Past Bosses (actually I learned a lot of what *not* to do, so I guess I did learn something)
- EINTLABSIL . . . from Dilbert.

Chapter 3

Everything I Needed to Learn about Business Strategy I Learned . . . from *Hell's Kitchen* and *Kitchen Nightmares*

I can tell in two minutes if I should hire someone in the kitchen. Two minutes. It's his desire. It's that open-eyed, attentive expression. If he doesn't have it . . . I mean, I can teach a chimp how to cook dinner. But I cannot teach a chimp how to love it.

—Mario Batali, *Esquire* (June 2004)

In the same way Mario Batali can tell a good chef in two minutes, good leaders tend to be good at spotting talented leaders. Both can see the internal passion versus someone going through the motions. So what does cooking have to do with business? Well, I couldn't write a book about business strategy and "secret sauce" without having a chapter on cooking, right? Therefore, we obviously need to talk about real sauces and the world of cooking. Can you name a bigger popular craze today than cooking? Take a look at your TV listings: *Hell's Kitchen*; *Kitchen Nightmares*; *Top Chef*; *Master Chef*; *Chopped*; *Iron Chef*; *Cutthroat Kitchen*; *Cake Boss*; *Ace of Cakes*; *Diners, Drive-Ins and Dives*; the list goes on and on. People, all kinds of people, are fascinated with gourmet cooking, home cooking, and competitive cooking. It's a dreamland for us eaters! Having said that, I need to state that I am a self-proclaimed foodie and amateur chef, emphasis on the amateur. So I find these shows inspiring and insightful for the cooking techniques and entertaining for the competitiveness, challenges, and mission-impossible timing and I like other episodes for some solid business savvy in the food world. Really? Business savvy, you say? Yes, absolutely! If you look past the Hollywood factor in these shows, you'll see some pretty insightful decision making and intelligence in running a business and competing. Let's look at two of my favorite shows, *Hell's Kitchen* and *Kitchen Nightmares* and break them down. Here is what you can learn about business from these two shows.

Hell's Kitchen

Competition brings out the best, and *Hell's Kitchen* is chock-full of competition. The show starts with one to two dozen chefs. Then week by week, host and Master Chef Gordon Ramsey throws out the worst chef or whoever didn't execute the best for a given week. Think of it like a weekly General Electric C-session (GE was notorious for having recurring employee ranking sessions and axing anyone who was a C). Ouch. But seriously, some of the chefs that come onto this show are green, like avocado green, and they need serious ripening. Over the course of several episodes, some folks do improve, and it's due to the level of competition. It's a survival of the fittest; Darwinism at its finest. Is business really any different? Consider a *Hell's* episode with 12 chefs. You have one or two front-runners—they are the lead dogs to catch. These folks usually are the full-meal deal. They have the cooking talent, but they also have the chops to communicate and build relationships with others. Next, you have two or three people at the cooking bottom; you know casting put them in the mix just to keep things entertaining due to their questionable piercings or extreme attitudes. Typically, the rest then fall into the middle of the pack. You'll get a couple of early flameouts, a couple of rising stars, a handful who never leave the middle of the pack, and a handful who couldn't cook a scallop to save their life! Wow. Business world—same thing. You have your market leader or leaders of two or three companies tops, your fast followers, your bottom of the heap, and the bell curve of companies in the middle who can't seem to differentiate, grow, innovate, or have the resources to rise to the top. But without a doubt, competition frames the market and landscape, and if you don't pay attention to the competition, you'll flame out early. Embrace the competition or it will eat your lunch!

An Incredible Sous-Chef Makes a Big Difference

Okay, I admit, I have a slight crush on Andi Van Willigan. Ever since my wife and I met her in Vegas on opening weekend of Gordon Ramsey's Steak at the Paris Las Vegas when she sat with us chatting over a glass of wine. Who is Andi Van Willigan? Are you kidding? She is the glue behind Gordon Ramsey. She is his confidante, his top lieutenant, his consigliore, his sous-chef. While you see Gordon cussing at the top of his lungs, Andi is in the background, driving, executing, planning, managing, and keeping Gordon up to speed on what is happening in the kitchen. This isn't said to diminish Gordon or his role, but his role would be different if he didn't have Andi as his chief operating officer, with her hand on the switch and executing his vision. Sound familiar? The greatest chefs in the world are similar to the greatest leaders/chief executive officers (CEOs). They have solid people behind them and more than likely one or two key lieutenants whom they trust with the keys to the Maserati, and for good reason. In a small company, you may be able to get away without having an Andi on your staff, but rest assured, in a midsize to large company, you need one or two to execute and deliver for your customers and to be a model driver to the rest of the executive team.

Know Your Sweet Spot

It's good to test your limits from time to time, else we never get better. But there is a wrong time/place and a right time/place to do this. In the *Hell's Kitchen* competition, chefs who stray too far from their comfort zone tend to get into trouble and may lose the challenge. It's hard to fault them, because they are striving and not being complacent. But everything should be a calculated risk, not a "shot in the dark" risk. You need to take risks, but you can't deviate so far from your sweet spot that you compromise your style, your values, or yourself. Play in your sweet spot, whether it's your market or your product niche, and if you are going to stray from that, seek advice and counsel and ensure your new endeavors make sense and that you can be successful. When businesses forget their sweet spots or take their eye off them to get into some new, totally different market or product niche, this can be a very risky decision and, more than likely, a poor choice.

Running the Pass

Gordon Ramsey is the expeditor; he runs the pass. (The pass is the name given to the physical division between the cooks and the waitstaff where food is "passed" between them.) The expeditor is shouting out orders based on incoming tickets, plating dishes to go out, and monitoring overall quality. That means he doesn't necessarily cook or prepare anything, but he is announcing orders, organizing, and commanding his brigade. His brigade is akin to your executive team. You need to be the one to orchestrate timing, ensuring everyone is prepared and executing together and that all stations are talking to one another. The CEO, like the expeditor, is responsible for timing, execution, adaptation, and ultimate success. The plate stops with you, and you need to ensure your customers are being taken care of with the experience they expect. Additionally, if one of your chefs is not managing their station properly and are bringing down the entire team, you may need to switch up responsibilities and re-divide work responsibilities or maybe even switch out a chef if required. The buck, or in this case, "the plate" stops with you and you are responsible.

Competing Restaurants

Restaurant competitions are a fun episode in *Hell's* and another well-known cooking show (see *Top Chef Restaurants Wars*). There are different varieties of this challenge, but at its most basic, chefs are challenged to envision a restaurant concept and menu and execute it for a night. One chef is normally in charge, and the others are to offer input and execute. Watching this is an entertaining *Harvard Business Review* on good, but more often bad, leadership examples. Some chefs are so blinded by finally having the opportunity and power over their team to create their baby, their first restaurant, that they lose their heads and don't lead as they should. They dictate tasks, don't listen to feedback, are blinded by their own ambitions, and can't get the other chefs to follow their personal dream. I hope that doesn't sound familiar, but unfortunately it probably does ring a bell from a past experience you may have had. This chef is the CEO who needs to take his or her vision, develop it with the other chefs, improve his or her own thinking with improved ideas from the other chefs, get them to buy in and own the restaurant concept, and then motivate them to execute. When you are the top chef of your business and need to execute your restaurant (business) concept, be sure you bring along the troops and keep them engaged in and bought in to your vision. All chefs, and leaders, have strengths and sweet spots and a good CEO will pull on those people at the right time to enhance and deliver on the companies' vision.

Perform Like a Champion

While *Hell's Kitchen* is a show itself, the true performance stage is the kitchen. Chefs spend hours prepping for the evening's service and getting ready for the onslaught of orders about to come their way. Preparation is crucial, no doubt. Having a plan is critical, or the kitchen staff will be running around like headless Cornish game hens. But execution and adaptiveness in the kitchen at showtime (dinnertime) is paramount. When the plans and prep go bad, you have to adapt. A good chef, just like a good leader, knows when to call an audible to the game plan and to edit the executional plan to achieve the intended results. You need to be able to work with the unpredictable—the stove that goes out, the produce that goes bad, the dish that just doesn't come together. These are all similar to strategies going bad during business execution. A good leader is like a good coach. A good coach makes a game plan and practices with the team. Then a great coach executes on game day and adjusts to situations that were not planned for. Prepare for the game, then play like a champion at showtime!

Kitchen Nightmares

Kitchen Nightmares is another Gordon Ramsey show, but with a slightly different twist. Rather than a cooking competition, a typical episode begins with a restaurant that was once great and is now in dire straits. Saving the restaurant will require the proverbial Hail Mary pass, throwing the ball deep into the end zone with two seconds left and hoping for a miracle. The restaurant's owners have run it aground and are out of money. Why is the situation so dire, and how can Gordon Ramsey fix it? The reasons why restaurants go downhill and how they need to be fixed are usually pretty straightforward. These shows are very entertaining, but you can predict what the issues are going to be after you see the opening scenes. The next sections provide typical Gordon Ramsey lessons and what he digs into. Look for the similarities to your business.

Know Your Customers, and Listen to Them

If I had a nickel for every time Gordon does a show where the restaurant owner thinks he understands his customer base but doesn't and totally runs the place into the ground, I would be able to add on a 2,000-bottle wine cellar to my house instead of 1,000. Typically these owners haven't really talked or, worse yet, listened to their customers in years. Gordon comes to a new town, walks around the streets for a couple hours, and finds out more information than the proprietor has ever gotten. It's not hard to know what your customers think, but you have to ask! And you need to listen constantly and consistently to your customers. The moment you think you know exactly what they want or you think the customers are "too dumb" to know what they want and *you* know better, game over.

Really, hotshot, you *don't* know it all. And while all the feedback may not be appropriate, it's your job to sift the wheat from the chaff. Ask your customers, listen to them, and check your ego at the door. Remember, they have a choice, and they are paying you for a product/service.

I Am the God of Food

This really goes hand in hand with the prior discussion of knowing your customer, but restaurateurs who think they are gods and their product rocks harder than anyone else's get into trouble. Think about the menu like you would a product portfolio. One dish/one product won't sustain a menu for long. And 100 variations get complicated, complex to execute, confusing to consumers, and are a nightmare to maintain. Keep it simple, keep it balanced, and reinvent yourself on a normal cycle. And recognize that you haven't cornered the market on absolutely every dish ever known to man and there could be better ones out there than yours. Good leaders will always be looking for ways to improve their offerings and not wait until they get told by the market. Think of this as a continuous cycle, not a destination that you reach and then stop at.

It's Not My Fault, They Didn't Tell Me!

Okay, the nickel rule from earlier applies here as well: I get a nickel every time I hear the phrase "They didn't tell me." Good grief. The statement usually begins with "The front of the house (dining room) is not listening to the back of the house (kitchen)." Or vice versa. Almost every nightmare episode has some sort of communication breakdown—the waitstaff didn't know the specials, the cook didn't know the customer feedback, the owner won't listen because he or she can't deal with problems, and the like. It's no different in business. Leadership isn't talking to line folks, line folks aren't giving feedback to leadership, and nobody is listening to the customers. Is it really that hard to talk to each other? It must be at times because not many people do it consistently or at least effectively. Finding the right ways to communicate so all are heard, people don't shut down, and feedback is communicated that is critical for success. And consistency is the recipe for success here. Communications is not a one-time event. Last, a rule of thumb on effective communications: You have two ears and one mouth. Use them in that proportion. It works better.

Not Managing the Details

Have you seen some of the food coolers Gordon walks into in these episodes? It makes you never want to go out to eat as long as you live. I've seen rotten lettuce and tomatoes, mice and rats, raw chicken with cooked chicken, mold balls, and unidentifiable things that I'm sure I'd puke at if I saw it live, which Gordon has done from time to time. So let's analyze this for a second. How hard is it to manage a cooler in a restaurant? Buy products, prep products, cook products, and sell products. Clean the cooler, and repeat and replenish as needed. Where does it run amuck? People not doing their jobs, the restaurant not having clear roles and responsibilities, someone who is disenfranchised or doesn't care or is improperly motivated and incentivized, or just simply a lack of supervision? Can you think of any business examples where the leader/supervisor isn't paying attention to the details and have let the "cooler" go to hell? Yes. It's easy to get complacent, but complacency also is easy to fix. You don't have to personally sweep the floors in your operation, but keep your eye on the details or they will come back to bite you. Keep your business organized, check in on the details, and hold people accountable.

Are You Tasting Your Food?

Many times Gordon will take a chef to task over seasoning. Usually the first question from his mouth is "Oh come on. Are you even tasting your food?" (spoken in a really defeated, almost whiny voice). Fact is, chefs needs to taste their food throughout the service and ensure some quality control. Business analogy: Are you using your own products? Same thing. If you are not regularly using your own products, shopping on your own Website, or calling your own customer service agents, then how do you know the quality of your products and the experience your customers are having? I've seen some really poor decisions by CEOs not to invest in portal development or experience programs or in some cases not even using their own products and services—can you imagine? You have to eat your own dog food before you ask your customers to pay to do so. The Golden Rule applies here: Treat others as you would like to be treated. Ensure you know how your clients and customers are being treated.

Simplicity and Its Impact on Execution

A common trap for many chefs is falling in love with their plates and techniques and wanting to show their culinary skills unnecessarily. Gordon explains how this happens with both seasoned chefs and newly minted ones. A chef who offers Gordon a 15-component signature dish that mixes six cooking styles and takes five minutes to explain the dish's name usually fails. Being simplistic in your food is not being simple. It is about being very deliberate and thoughtful and letting the food speak for itself. Do you see the parallel to business, specifically to product development? Sometimes businesses put so many bells and whistles on their products that they lose the core value proposition and become unmanageable. That has a huge ripple effect. Sales has to take longer to sell a more complicated product, manufacturing time to market is longer due to complexity, customer service training and call handling are longer with more escalations due to complexity, and customer satisfaction is likely to be lower as people have more questions on how to use the complicated product. Simple is not being simplistic, but it *is* about being smart and thoughtful in your delivery such that products are intuitive for your customers.

Counting Coins in the Kitchen

As a chef, you are the artist, right? You create plates for the palate, and customers swoon over your creations. You leave the back-office details to others to manage. Okay, good luck. In *Kitchen Nightmares*, this is a typical pitfall. Chefs or owners are so full of themselves and their creations, the hell with cost control. They want top service so they overstaff. They want happy diners so they give free drinks and appetizers. None of these things are inherently bad, once in a while. But consistently doing these things and not paying attention to balance and fiscal controls makes you the latest restaurant to be out of business. There is an obvious analogy to running a business and needing ongoing and tight fiscal controls. But in a business, this task is normally done by the chief financial officer (CFO). Typically, it is up to the CFO to be the fiscal disciplinarian; others are left to run and execute business plans. To some degree this is okay; it's a check and balance of controls. But the CFO can't be the only person with financial discipline. If he or she is, the CFO is always the "no" person. Many times CFOs should be focused on investments for growth, efficiency, and innovation. But if they are dedicated disciplinarians, who is making the strategic financial decisions? Make leaders responsible for their individual budgets, and don't leave it all up to the CFO to monitor.

Final Plating of This Chapter

I hope the foodies reading this book enjoyed the comparisons of fine business strategy with fine dining. Like a final plate going out to a hungry customer, here I put a final touch on this chapter. Having had a couple of cooking positions during my college years and some more recent education at Le Cordon Bleu culinary college, I know that there is one key advantage in being a chef that you normally don't get in the business world: instantaneous feedback. When customers don't like your plate, you hear about it from them via a returned plate to the kitchen or a waiter who gives you the feedback, sometimes in a not-so-nice tone. The good chef will take the feedback and improve and adapt instantly so that the next plate that goes out does not have the same problem. Often feedback in the business world is not this expedient, but feedback is key and preparation enables execution. So think of the kitchen parables and remember:

- **Run the pass (your business) effectively and efficiently.** Think of Gordon Ramsey running the pass, not compromising quality, clearly communicating responsibilities, and organizing and driving the team.
- **Simplicity and attention to detail.** Manage the details behinds the scenes (operational excellence) and have simplicity in your entrée (your product) such that it can be executed flawlessly and let the core ingredients shine. Don't get caught up in unnecessary food components (infamous bells and whistles on a product).
- **Taste your own food.** Don't ever send out your plate without tasting the food—a cardinal sin in cooking. Same with your products. If you are not using them or experiencing them as a customer would, why are you asking someone else to pay money to do so? Test your own products, eat your own food, and make sure it's worthy of a five-star rating.

Summary

Conclusion. Keep your "cooler" clean, organized, and stocked. After picking the right restaurant and menu (business value proposition and strategy), the key to winning is successfully managing and executing the details.

Gold nuggets you took away to share with your board of directors or your staff, or for personal reflection:

1. _____

2. _____

Additional Resources/Tools

Watch any show from any season from the programs discussed in this chapter. You're bound to learn business lessons and be entertained. Watch for the common themes and see if you can predict what Gordon is going to do before he does.

Check out www.ForeSee.com. Customer experience is critical. Check ForeSee's value prop and tools for customer experience and analytics. Half of the Fortune 100 measure customer experience with ForeSee, and it may help you crowdsource ideas.

Cook your favorite family recipe. Seriously! Cooking can be very therapeutic, and how often in business do you get to see instant results like a finished dish from your actions? Have a little fun!

Chapter 4

Everything I Needed to Learn about Business Strategy I Learned . . . at the Movies

You know what your problem is, it's that you haven't seen enough movies—all of life's riddles are answered in the movies.

—Steve Martin

Parables have been used for centuries to pass down stories, wisdom, truths, and other information deemed valuable. A story or parable is simply easier to remember than a set of facts or figures.

Hollywood has been telling stories for years via the movies. Some of these movies are purely for entertainment, and others have some lessons included—whether you picked them out or not. If you ask people to name their favorite movie and why, you get to know something about that person. Almost everyone has a favorite movie that they find entertaining, exciting, or inspiring.

21 Movies: Six Lessons on Business Strategy

In this chapter, I describe some of my favorite movies; movies that have lessons on business strategy. Run through the list, relate to them, learn what you can from them, but, most important, file them in the back of your mind and remember these scenes and morals for a future time when you will need them.

Passion/Motivation

Good businesses begin with someone's dream. It takes someone's passion and motivation to create something, to make something better, or create something that nobody even understands the need for.

1. **Mission Impossible II.** There is a great scene early in the movie between Ethan Hunt and his boss.

Ethan's boss is explaining the mission to Hunt, who is deciding if he should choose to accept it. Hunt is upset by a detail and says, "I don't think I can get her to do it [part of the mission]. It will be difficult." His boss responses, "That is why they call it mission impossible, Mr. Hunt. Mission difficult should be a walk in the park for you." **Moral:** Know your mission, go after it with a vengeance, and recognize that if it were easy, anyone could do it. Running a business is not easy, but it is not impossible.

2. *Hunt for Red October.* This is my all-time favorite movie. I love the movie's strategy and plot. It's worth a Saturday afternoon or evening if you haven't seen it. Sean Connery is the best. In the captain's room scene with all his executive officers, Captain Marko Ramius informs the men of the letter he sent to their Soviet command announcing his intention to defect. The officers didn't know he had done this, and an argument ensues. They had jointly planned to defect, but they didn't count on the entire Soviet submarine contingent trying to hunt them down in the process. They ask Ramius why he would do such a thing. His response? A parable. He tells them, "You see, when Cortés had arrived at the New World, he knew it would be difficult to establish a colony and some may want to return home. So he burned the ships to motivate his crew to succeed. There would be no going

back." **Moral:** I'm not suggesting you burn your ships and take on a crazy new path in business, but sometimes motivation is needed. The burning platform of "if we don't succeed, our business may die" is a powerful motivator. When you make a decision in business, make it a commitment, and don't turn back unless new circumstances dictate a change.

3. *Hidalgo.* Viggo Mortensen as Frank Hopkins races his "painted horse," a wild mustang, across the Arabian desert in the great horse race. The entire movie embodies will and passion. **Moral:** You *can* overcome great odds and stick it to your competitors when they scoff at you if you have the knowledge, will, and passion to keep at it. And a little help along the way doesn't hurt either. Don't be too proud to accept the "butter from a camel's milk" when it is offered.

4. *Secretariat.* Secretariat was an American Thoroughbred racehorse that in 1973 became the first U.S. Triple Crown champion in 25 years. He set race records in all three events in the series: the Kentucky Derby (1:59), the Preakness Stakes (1:53), and the Belmont Stakes (2:24)—records that still stand. Yeah, kinda good, I'd say. This movie is an inspiring story of the passion of one woman and her belief in her horse, Secretariat, defying all the odds. **Moral:** If the odds makers got it right all the time, they wouldn't be working folks. And if you ignore the intangibles, whether it's

a horse or a business deal, you are not looking at the full picture and may get left in the dust. Look beyond the obvious and invest in people as well as their companies; it could be a good bet.

5. *A Knight's Tale.* This is probably my second favorite movie. It's funny, witty, adventurous, and at times a tearjerker. There is a scene where a poor, simple father asks a nobleman to mentor his son so the boy can have a better life. The father tells his son to "change his stars." When the son returns to see his father later in life, he has done just that. **Moral:** It's not enough just to dream about changing your stars; you have to go out and actually do it. I am firm believer that opportunities don't just come to you; you create them. Don't keep saying next year, next season, maybe someday. Be like "Sir William" and go out and seize those dreams!

6. *Annapolis.* Similar to *A Knight's Tale*, this is a movie about defying odds, proving yourself to others (and to yourself), and pursuing your dreams. Jake Huard is a typical kid going through a maturation process in a tough environment without a lot of support, but he followed a dream and stubbornly refuses to quit. **Moral:** Don't let anyone tell you that you can't achieve something. And when you feel like you have nothing left to give on certain days, reach down a find just a little bit more and know that you left it all on the field for the day.

Imagination/Innovation

Now that we have proper motivation, let's talk about adding a little imagination and innovation. Here are two movies that embody this theme the best.

7. *Matrix.* The plot of this movie, being inside a computer program and doing things bound only by "computer rules and code," is incredible. Neo's mind in the sparring room with Morpheus is taxed as he needs to reprogram his thinking for what is possible in the matrix. **Moral:** It's hard to think outside the box sometimes. In business, at times, there are game changers, big trends in which the world of business changes—think of the creation of the Internet. Sometimes you have to break reality and get past what is possible or conceivable today to see the future. Easier said than done.

8. *Avatar.* I thought the technical delivery of this movie was astonishing. Really, motion picture development has come a long, long way. To me, it's not the movie itself that is intriguing but its innovative, game-changing evolution of computer animated graphics. This was a serious advance forward due to a handful of people who imagined it, innovated it, pursued it, and executed it. **Moral:** Change is inevitable. But someone has to dream it, cogitate on it, design it, test it, fail at it, and then ultimately succeed at it. If you are going to put your industry on its ear with big change, then

think big, think about a whole new way of executing and delivering on your value proposition. Imagine it, and innovate around it.

Planning

Okay, so we have passion, we have some imagination. How exactly are we going to plan for and deliver on our business? The next four movies are examples of complex, thoughtful, careful planning. Next time you are creating a plan to execute a strategy, use the planning in these movies as your benchmark and think about whether you *really* planned the business strategy out.

9. ***Ocean's Eleven***, ***Twelve***, and ***Thirteen***. I love these movies! The planning of the original Vegas heist, the turns and plot twists in the Fabergé egg job in *Twelve*, and the planning in Reuben's revenge job in *Thirteen* are all extraordinary. Hollywood, of course. But the planning, timing, and execution depicted is fabulous to watch. **Moral:** Almost any job is possible with proper planning and identification of clear roles and responsibilities. In each of these movies, the master thieves do dry runs of the heists, and each person describes their role, where they will be at such and such time, and how they plan to execute their task. It's planning the job down to the fine print, including contingencies.

10. *The Shooter.* The general plot is an ex-gunnery sergeant is helping the CIA prevent a presidential assassination. He must plan how he would kill the president in order for it to be prevented. Then he proceeds to conduct his due diligence and plan the mission. While there is much more to this story, the planning of the assassination amid all the variables is the takeaway here. **Moral:** Make your plan. Then consider all the variables. Have you accounted for all the variables—in the film it includes humidity, wind, angle, and others—for the shot to be effective? Conclusions and results become easier to achieve when you have laid out a proper plan.

11. *Apollo 13.* This film is about a plan (landing on the moon again) that quickly went south. The movie is really about the secondary plan to get the astronauts back home safely while dealing with one issue after another. **Moral:** The best-laid plans, by the smartest people in the world, can still go to hell sometimes. When that does happen, you need to respond quickly, decisively, and with as much information as possible. Think about how the flight controller, Gene Krantz, responded and drove the NASA staff to find a solution to get his astronauts back home. He operated with as many facts as possible, then made choices. He asked for opinions and options, then made new plans.

12. *Italian Job.* This movie provides multiple planning examples about getting the job done. I especially

like the opening scene of lifting the building in Venice (later dubbed "the Italian Job") and planning this heist. Charlie is the master planner in pulling off the heists in these movies. Just this past year, I was in Venice with my family, and we saw the building where they shot this scene—amazing! (and I really miss the daily intake of gelato). **Moral:** You need a plan, the right assets to pull off the plan, and contingency plans, and freakish execution. Charlie's team didn't have a safe cracker for their mission, and they needed to recruit for it, so they did. After you have laid out your plan, do you have all the assets to pull off the job?

Values and Teamwork

We have passion and innovation, and now we have planned our job. It's going to take a team to execute our strategy. There is no such thing as a one-man show; everyone needs a team—direct, indirect, virtual, or otherwise. We all partner with others to deliver on our business models. Many of us want to move forward with people with similar values. If we are to succeed, we need our partners to succeed. How do we know our collective values? Consider these film examples:

13. *It's a Wonderful Life.* Can you think of another movie known by more people that tugs at your heartstrings and makes you think about your true

north direction in life? **Moral:** Know your true north, don't forget where you come from, and remember what is important in life.

14. *The Bucket List.* How could I not have a Jack Nicholson movie on my list? I'd fear risk of a repeat of the shower scene from the *Shining* if I don't include him. If you haven't seen *The Bucket List*, it's a must-see. The entire movie is about the meaning of life, friendships, and family. Jack and Morgan Freeman are perfectly paired and really make you think about life and choices made. **Moral:** The moral in this movie and its application to our discussion is simple: Know what you want out of life, don't get sidetracked in the urgent unimportant stuff, else 30 years will go by and you'll have a lot of regrets. Hold true to your values and don't sacrifice them.

15. *Miracle.* Another great sports movie, especially when you consider this is a true story. There are many great scenes in this movie, including an inspirational talk before the face-off with the Russians. But the scene we are going to discuss is much closer to the opening of the film. It's when Herb Brooks is interviewing for the job as head coach with a roomful of people peppering him with questions and largely not listening to his responses. At one point they get sidetracked and begin discussing the team's dismal odds and especially what could happen if they face the Russians after their National Hockey League all-star team just got its butt kicked by them.

Herb begins to put his things away and mutters, "You didn't lose because you didn't have enough talent." He proceeds to explain that "all-star" teams fail because they are collection of individual stars and don't function as a team. The Russians win because they take their talent and use it in a system for the betterment of the entire team. **Moral:** Having the right team is obviously important, but how they work together is as important, if not more so, as what they can each independently accomplish. Next time you are going to add someone to your executive team, or any team for that matter, think about how the team will be affected. Will it get stronger as a whole? Or are you adding an all-star player who will suboptimize the other team members?

16. *Friday Night Lights*. If you played high school football on Friday nights like I did, you get this movie. Especially Texas football. It's a simplistic movie plot about a team of high school boys and their quest for a football championship in Texas. One problem that gets in their way: Boobie Miles gets hurt. Boobie is their star running back, and their team revolves around him. He is their greatest strength and also their biggest vulnerability. Without Boobie, they are a different team with different odds. **Moral:** One person does not make a team. Similarly, you can't run a business around one person. This happens many times with entrepreneurs. Yes, entrepreneurs need to get a company up and going, but they need to bring in additional talent and a

team to fill other roles at some point. If your business revolves around one key leader, one critical engineer, one crack sales guy, one indispensable person, you have big risk.

17. *Hoosiers.* This is one of the best sports films that teaches the importance of teamwork. Coach Norman Dale is masterful at setting boundaries, providing his team the basics and not gimmicks, administering discipline, and inspiring the boys to greatness. **Moral:** Anything is achievable with the right team, the right coach, and direction and execution. Extreme, unselfish teamwork trumps a great deal of other factors.

18. *Armageddon.* Let's get past the premise of this movie that the earth is going to be decimated by an asteroid and get to the application to business strategy. The scene is when Harry Stamper learns of his challenge to help the government destroy the asteroid. Harry begins recruiting his team for the mission. He narrates for moviegoers who each member is while he is recruiting them. Let's just say these guys are some colorful cats. This is their normal oil drilling team—they have been in the muck together for many years as a group and they know how to pull together and get a job done. **Moral:** Team, team, team. When you look at the team members individually, you say, really? Are you kidding? But these guys know how each other works, what they can and can't do, and how to pull together to get results. In business, and specifically with execution, it's not about

having the dream team of business MVPs to plan and execute; it's about having the *right* team of individuals who can work together to achieve tremendous results—more so than what they could have achieved individually and simply added together. Good teams create synergies.

Customer Experience

If you are not working on things that your customers will love, not just like, but love, what are you doing? When you think of movies and a scene where one person shows he'll do anything to keep his client, this is the only example needed.

19. *Jerry McGuire.* You know the phrase even if you haven't seen the movie. "*Show me the money!*" And that is the scene to learn from. Jerry McGuire will do whatever it takes, including shouting "Show me the money" at the top of his lungs to his client in order to make him happy. How many of us are willing to do something like this for our customers? **Moral:** Without customers, you don't have a business. Maybe public humiliation is going a bit far to show customers you love them, but you had better be thinking of how you can show customers you care about them, you are listening to them, and their business is important to you. Else you are going to lose them to someone who will take care of them.

Knowing Your Market/Strategic Intel

When we are too inwardly focused, we are partially blind. Sometimes we become so obsessed with our businesses that we think we know the market without actually consulting the market and checking in. Consider these movies and how they did/didn't react to market changes and new facts:

20. *Toy Story II.* The scene is when Tour Guide Barbie is driving around Woody, Mr. Potato Head, and Hamm in her car at Al's Toy Barn. She is giving the boys a tour when she hits the Buzz Lightyear aisle. During this PG movie for kids, but laced with adult-entertaining clean one-liners, she explains why there are rows and rows of Buzz Lightyear figures. Tour Guide Barbie tells them, "Back in 1995 shortsighted retailers did not order enough dolls to meet demand." This is a joke and a fact: When the original *Toy Story* was released, toy sellers did not think the movie would be a hit, and they indeed did not order enough dolls to keep up with demand. This sequel to the original movie pokes a little fun at that. **Moral:** Take it from Tour Guide Barbie: Don't get caught flatfooted in operations and misinterpret product demand. Plan multiple scenarios of volumes and have contingencies for explosive growth and how you could deal with it.

21. *National Treasure.* If you like a witty adventure movie that makes you think along the way,

watch *National Treasure*. It's a thrill ride of clues and adventures en route to finding a treasure beyond belief. What is impressive in this story is the application of problem solving and creative thinking based on information. Every time Benjamin Franklin Gates gets a new clue, he has to figure out the solution, then plan and execute how to get to the next stage and procure the next puzzle piece. He is constantly problem solving based on the newest information. **Moral:** Strategic intelligence in our industry and other applicable information is very important. However, information without action is meaningless. The real art and leadership is knowing which information to listen to, how to react and adapt to that information, and how to execute your next steps.

The Final Scene

Yes, there are many other great movies out there, and many that have morals and life lessons that could be applied to business strategy. I hope some of these resonated with you and made you think of even more examples from your own movie favorites. Next time you sit down with a bucket of popcorn, challenge yourself to look for business strategy lessons from the movie around passion, innovation, planning, teamwork, and customer experience and strategic intelligence. Consider how they apply to your current business situation and whether there is a parable to be told to your staff on Monday.

Summary

Conclusion. When we oversimplify and think of "business strategy," we think of the planning aspect. Yes, planning is very important, as highlighted by a handful of movies in this chapter. But you need to first start with passion, motivation, and innovation and then take that planning and executing through your value system, with knowledge, and teamwork to win the Oscar.

Gold nuggets you took away to share with your board of directors and your staff, or for personal reflection:

1. _____
2. _____

Additional Resources/Tools

Watch any of the 21 movies listed. Enjoy and watch for the described scenes and more.

Executing through your value system. Bill George is a fantastic leader, writer, and person. I'd highly recommend his book *Authentic Leadership*, if you haven't read it already. Bill will help you consider and hopefully find, your true north.

Conduct a hedgehog strategy session, as described in Jim Collins's book *Good to Great.* The six lessons from the movies in this chapter could be consolidated or redefined as Collins's three parts of a successful hedgehog strategy. Have you identified your business's sweet spot?

Chapter 5

Everything I Needed to Learn about Business Strategy I Learned ... Growing Up on a Farm

Opportunity is missed by most people because it is dressed in overalls and looks like work.
—Thomas Alva Edison

This is a bit of a tough-love chapter for me. There are many lessons learned in this chapter that I didn't realize for years to come. In many ways, it's a typical story of a kid maturing. You think you have all the answers, only to get older and more experienced and learn just how little you really know about life. For me, my father's occupation of farming was the framework for many lessons to be learned later in life.

As a boy, I hated farming. I thought I could do much more than that and couldn't believe my father enjoyed it. He could never vacation, he never appeared to be having much fun, and it eventually cost him his life through sickness at the young age of 58. Unfortunately, his eldest son, my brother, followed in his footsteps and met with similar consequences. He died four months after my father at the age of 31 after a battle with cancer. Hence I was bitter about farming and blamed it for what it did to my family for years to come. I did not look for lessons learned, but wanted to move on and away from this horrible past. Now, being a bit older, wiser, and at least a little more reflective, I can look back objectively and give you some lessons learned from farming and how they apply to business strategy and execution. I didn't see them at the time, but I do now. Those years on the farm taught me more than most books.

Hard Work

Hard work is the most obvious, so let's start with it. People use phrases like "nose to the grindstone" or "working in the salt mines" to explain hard work. More colorful people may use a phrase like "shoveling shit." Have you ever shoveled shit? I mean literally. I have. It's through this unglamorous yet necessary task on a farm that I really appreciated and understood the value of going to college. I didn't really care to shovel shit the rest of my life. Having said that, I think everyone should have to do this at some point in life; it builds a little character.

Whatever the job, everyone should have to spend some time in a shoveling shit–type job to have an appreciation for hard work and the inherent good feeling that comes from a hard day's work. Look at people who are tired at the end of the day, and they are usually pretty satisfied. Enough said.

Being the Boss

One of the greatest aspects of being a farmer is you are your own boss and control your destiny. But if you don't get up and milk those cows, bail that hay, fix that fence line, it's not going to get done. I didn't really appreciate the entrepreneurial spirit my father had; only now can I see that. I realized later that I learned this entrepreneurial spirit from him early, when I was about 10 years old.

Our farm was on a lake in a small town in Minnesota: Lake Aaron. In the summer, this lake and several around it were popular, small-town destinations for vacationers to get away from the city, do a little fishing, maybe drink a beer or two, and enjoy the starry nights. The road that passed our farmhouse went to these lakes. So at some point that I don't remember we began to sell worms for fishing to the vacationers. I know that my older brother Willie and sister Nancy did this for a spell, but when I came up the bottom of the ranks, the worm business fell to me. It was my first youthful dealings in being an entrepreneur, being responsible, and delivering to customers. *The following* are the basic learnings from a simple worm business that are lessons learned for any business:

- **Take care of your customers and they'll take care of you.** Why was this a thriving little worm business? Because people got what they wanted, and repeat business was huge. Give people a good product (fresh worms, not half decayed) at a good price, and they'll come back. Does it get any simpler than this?
- **The market sets the price, and customer service drives intangible value.** When new people would see the "Worms for Sale" sign and stop in the first time, they were always amazed to hear the price of 50 cents for 50 worms. They knew it would have been far higher in a bait shop in a larger town. In the years we did this little business, I don't recall many times getting only 50 cents. People

recognized the value, saw a good deal, and rewarded the worm digger with the price of the product and a tip for entrepreneurialism. Sure, I could have raised the price, and maybe I should have, but my parents were teaching me value, hard work, and customer service. Actually, the unsolicited tips were far more exciting than getting paid the 50 cents in the first place.

- **Consistency.** Sometimes I didn't feel like digging worms in advance of a big weekend when I knew customers would be coming by. After all, there was hay to bail, cows to milk, and, yes, more shit to shovel. So sometimes digging more worms, although it meant money to a young kid, was just not going to happen. Then customers would show up for worms, not stopping at multiple other bait shops along the way, only to get to me and find that I had no inventory. Ouch. Now what were they supposed to do? Drive all this way to go fishing, grab some bait at their favorite vendor, and hit the lake. But now, no bait. That hurts on the ol' customer retention and satisfaction ratings. Lesson learned.

- **Keep your overhead low.** Pretty basic rule in business, even in digging worms. This was a low-cost, low-overhead business. We dug worms in our woods, refrigerated them in the house in an old refrigerator, used a "For Sale" sign made and given to us by my godfather, Hubert, and used peach cans to package the worms for customers. In retrospect, the peach cans were key. Think about what packaging costs and also about recycling programs in big businesses. I was taking a discarded good (peach cans) in our house of two parents and seven kids and recycling long before it was in vogue. Even more green than that was when customers would return for more worms and bring back their old worm cans, saying "Fill 'er up." I was green and didn't even know it! I could have had fancy packaging, bigger signs, maybe company pens (okay, that would have been a bit much), but I kept overhead low and margins high by providing the basics.

These were some of the lessons learned from a small but thriving worm business as a kid. What was your first entrepreneurial adventure and what lessons do you remember?

Planning and Executing

I didn't recognize any of these business lessons until years later. Think about the planning and execution that goes into planting crops, fertilizing and cultivating them, and harvesting them. It's a lot of work and with a slow cycle of seeing the fruits of our labor.

Just planning a day in general on the farm was a task. The normal chores of milking, cattle management and feeding, milk pickup, and machinery repair.

How do you plan your day and get everything done? My dad never had a to-do list; how did he keep track of anything? Guess it was all in his head, and he didn't overplan, he just did it. Poor execution in the spring and summer months showed up in the fall harvest. Poor planning left tasks undone and created risks. Imagine a fence that needed repair not getting done and cattle escaping. Have you ever gotten pulled out of bed at 2 a.m. to chase cows that escaped due to a break in the fence? It's not fun.

Technology

Technology on the farm—boy, it has come a long way. When I was growing up, we carried buckets of milk and dumped them into what was called a step-saver, which then took the milk to the bulk tank for holding until the milk truck came. Before that, in my dad's day, he milked totally by hand. Want to know which old farmers milked by hand? Look at the size of their fingers; they are like Polish sausages from milking all day long!

Pitchforks for shoveling manure were replaced by skid loaders. Manure spreaders were replaced by manure pits that self-pump into the fields to fertilize crops. (If you are not a farmer and think I'm kidding, I'm not.) Old single-row planters were replaced with GPS-aided planters that cost more than five times my first house. Technological advances came in spurts and changed the old family farm concept into big business. Smaller farmers who didn't have the technology and scale found it hard to keep up and be cost competitive. *The* same challenges in many businesses.

Is there any business that isn't impacted by changes in technology? Not many. Manufacturers always have smart industrial engineers running around doing process improvement and improving equipment. Small-business owners add an ancillary device onto their iPhone to take credit card payments in three seconds so customers can pay by credit versus cash. Businesses use complex software and systems for methodologies and services. Almost all of us use some form of technology, and keeping up with that technology and identifying fads from game changers in its use is an imperfect science.

Milk Co-ops

When I was a kid, the milk truck came to the farm every two days to empty our milk tank. The driver took our milk and milk from all the other local farmers to the co-op, where it was processed and sold. Milk checks were sent to the farm, after deductions for feed, seed, fertilizer, and other items that had been purchased through the co-op. What I didn't realize back then was the power of a co-op. That co-op allowed us to get better pricing on our milk due to economies of scale and joining forces with other farmers. We do the same thing in business. We have purchasing co-ops to get better pricing to compete with bigger companies that have the clout to negotiate their own deals. I'd lump joint ventures into this bucket as well since they are about two entities coming together to create synergies and ask: What are you doing in your business that may be better served through a joint venture, or where could you get better economics through joint purchasing practices? Milk co-ops are a simple example of market economics.

Innovation

I'd suggest that almost all farmers are innovators due to either their nature or their need to survive. Actually my father-in-law, Al, is like this. He and his two brothers run one of the largest dairy farms in Minnesota. Their cows have radio frequency identification tags, which keep track of data for each cow, including how many gallons of milk she gives. The milking floors rise up and down to adjust to the required height and optimize the milking process.

There are GPS systems that guide planters and keep track of farm equipment's location and maintenance, and mobile device alert systems that warn of things such as low oil or a roaming tractor. There are tons of crazy technological advances, at least to this small farm boy. But simply buying the latest and greatest equipment is not enough. In the case of my father-in-law, Al is continuously customizing their farm's equipment, innovating it to make it more efficient based on his experience, or outright inventing new solutions. Many farmers do this out of necessity to save some dollars on expensive repairs; others like Al simply are innovators and know how to tweak and invent things to make them better or solve a need.

Do you know any businesses that don't talk about innovation or the need to innovate? Not many. Actually, innovation as a word is used so frequently it has lost some of its meaning. Going back to our earlier discussion on innovation, it's a core part of success in just about any business. Innovate or die. Regardless, every business needs to innovate, just as the farmer does. You need to innovate around continuous process improvements to make the day-to-day work more efficient; you also need to innovate on a larger, grander scale, like the farmer's technological advances I named earlier, to drive cost competitiveness and effectiveness.

Outsourcing

You may be doing some head-scratching on this point: Outsourcing on a farm? Really, what is he talking about? Like most other farms, on our small farm, we planted grain to use as cattle feed. But we didn't plant a significant amount of grain, only enough for feed. Farmers need a machine called a combine to harvest grain when it is ready.

Do you know how much a grain combine costs? It simply was not cost effective to buy a combine for that one time per year it was required and for such a low volume. Therefore, we hired a neighbor each fall to combine our grain for us. Many farmers like to be independent and have this type of equipment for themselves, so this was a little out of the norm, but it was good business and good economics by my father.

The cost–benefit analysis just wasn't there to buy a combine. I'm positive my dad did not prepare an Excel spreadsheet with a sensitivity analysis and multi-scenario model with crop yields to make this decision; he did it in his head. Actually, Excel didn't even exist yet, nor even Lotus 1-2-3 or Quattro Pro! Remember Quattro Pro spreadsheets? Sorry, I digress. The recovering accountant in me comes out from time to time. Businesses don't have to be large to outsource certain activities; as a matter of fact, you can argue that smaller businesses have lower volumes and resources in general so it is usually more cost effective to buy these services rather than invest fully in them. What should you be outsourcing?

Delegation

When you are a farmer, there is no shortage of chores to do. And normally, it's up to you to get them done. Hence the family farm. Dads needed some help, and having Ma and the kids help with the chores was an expected part of living on the farm. However, sometimes pride can get in the way, and you feel not all jobs can be delegated. You may have heard of the quote "You should only delegate jobs that you have done or would do yourself" (i.e., don't ask someone to do something you wouldn't).

This was never my dad's issue; his issue was delegating and trusting others to do the big stuff. The big stuff on a farm is milking the cows. If you can't delegate milking to someone else from time to time, a hired hand or neighbor, you are doomed to do it yourself, every day, twice or three times a day with no relief. Is your business any different? If you can't trust the operations of the business to someone, even for a night, then you may have not built a solid, stable business. If the entire business runs around you, what happens when something happens to you? Delegation is not a sign of weakness; it is a sign of strength.

Sharpening the Saw

As Stephen Covey has taught many, you need to be able to "sharpen the saw" and keep yourself in good health, good spirits, and with a balance in life and from time to time reinvent yourself. I thought my dad was terrible at this. He was work, work, work, and that was all that seemed to matter. He could rarely leave the farm, because who else would milk the cows? Interestingly enough, as I look back, yes, my father worked very hard. But he actually did do some sharpening of the saw activities, and I just didn't realize it.

As I was the youngest of seven kids, my father was a bit older when I came along. But I remember as a young boy going into town with my dad and he playing softball once a week with the guys, mostly other farmers. But more than anything else, my father loved to fish. Our farmland included lakeshore and 24/7 access to the best fishing lake I've encountered in my life. For the most part, we didn't even have a boat so we used our uncle Jim's. Nor did we regularly have a motor. We would row out in the boat to go fishing. Not exactly big-time fishing with bass boats, 200-horsepower Mercurys, and rapala sponsorships; we rowed out in a 14-foot something and fished with worms from our woods. This is my best childhood memory: fishing with my dad and cleaning the fish afterward. My mother would help clean too, and after a successful outing the three of us would sit in the kitchen cleaning fish late at night. We would race to see who could clean more. I didn't see it then, but I do now; this was sharpening of the saw for my father, and it worked for him. Whatever it takes to rejuvenate you and replenish your core to get back to work, you need to find it and *do it* regularly. It's important and not to be overlooked.

Summary

Conclusion. Hard work is required in any business, period. So get to it!

Gold nuggets you took away to share with your board of directors or your staff, or for personal reflection:

1. _____

2. _____

Additional Resources/Tools

Read up on Howard Buffett, the son of legendary investor Warren Buffett. Howie, as he is known, has been chosen to succeed Warren as chairman of Berkshire Hathaway. A farmer, Howie is no chip off the old block and is said to be more comfortable on a tractor than in a boardroom. He also is a hands-on philanthropist whose foundation spends $50 million per year to combat world hunger—nice. This guy is worth a read.

Pick up a Zebco closed reel (an open spool can tangle easily for novice fishermen and ruin the day) and fishing pole from Cabella's or Gander Mountain. They cost about $50 to $100. Memories and self-sharpening time? Priceless.

Go do some hard labor. I'm not kidding. When is the last time you mowed your own lawn (not hard labor, but close enough), shoveled a driveway full of snow, or chopped wood? A little hard labor can remind us of the trials that we have gone through along the way.

Chapter 6

Everything I Needed to Learn about Business Strategy I Learned . . . from the Bible

Just as a candle cannot burn without fire, men cannot live without a spiritual life.

—The Buddha

What is the most published book in history?

Black Beauty, published in 1877	50 million copies	No
Charlotte's Web, published in 1952	45 million copies	No
The Lord of the Rings, published in 1954–55	150 million copies	No
A Tale of Two Cities, published in 1859	200 million copies	No

Of course you know the answer: the Bible, with 2.5 billion copies! Consider this: If the Bible is the most copied and published work in the history of the world, do you think there may be some gold nuggets in there on how to succeed in life? Success can mean many different things, but certainly the Bible contains a plethora of parables to teach you life lessons and things to pay attention to. Regardless of your religious affiliation, consider this a little objective research, not a religious statement. I'd much prefer to talk about faith than religion, as I believe in the first and struggle with the latter, but that is a different book. Suspend your judgment temporarily on this topic and review the quotations, which come from pens of men inspired thousands of years ago. See if the five categories and 20 verses from scripture offer something of value that applies to our current business world. Before we discuss the categories, consider this opening verse as a foundation for all:

> Whoever walks in integrity walks securely, but whoever takes crooked paths will be found out.
> **—Proverbs 10:9**

Business leaders who have been in the trenches have gone through crucibles, have seen ups and downs, and will talk about integrity. Sometimes they will talk about choices they wish they could make again; others, where they reflect on a difficult choice made with integrity. From a business standpoint, I think you can measure integrity by these things: repeat business, client retention, growth, employee tenure, and employee and customer satisfaction. Taking "crooked paths" always comes back to bite you. As you read these parts of scripture and business corollaries, do it with a foundation of integrity.

Five Themes of Business Parables from the Bible

A friend of mine once said that you can take just about any Bible verse and, used out of context, make it mean whatever you want. I agree that things taken out of context can be manipulated. Which is why rather than taking one or two verses and preaching on them, I like to offer five themes taken from multiple verses and look at themes and correlations and then apply that to business strategy and management.

Vision/Planning

Restating a comment from Chapter 4, businesses start with a vision. And then someone sat down and created some sort of plan, even if just on the back of a cocktail napkin. Having a vision and thinking through the first few steps are just the beginning.

> The LORD answered me and said, "Record the vision and inscribe it on tablets, that the one who reads it may run."
>
> **—Habakkuk 2:2**

When the entire team understands and is part of the vision and mission setting, that team can run like the wind. All members are working toward the same end. If vision is unclear, execution will be unclear and goals will not be attained.

> Where there is no vision, the people are unrestrained.
>
> **—Proverbs 29:18**

A business needs clear goals and boundaries. I like to think of setting parameters using the analogy of sailing. When you sail, you tack back and forth to get to your destination. It's not a straight, exact path but a process. Business is the same. Yes, the shortest distance between two points is a straight line, but business is seldom that straightforward, and you need to have puts and takes to get to your objectives and goals. But without a vision of where you are going and some guideposts, you'll never reach your destination.

> Through presumption comes nothing but strife, but with those who receive counsel is wisdom.
>
> **—Proverbs 13:10**

Clarifying direction is critical. There is no disgrace in clarifying direction. Disgrace and falls can occur due to lack of clarity and not seeking confirmation. A wise person consistently checks a compass to ensure he or she is on the right path. Check frequently, don't assume and presume!

> The plans of the diligent lead surely to advantage, but everyone who is hasty comes surely to poverty.
>
> **—Proverbs 21:5**

Plan, then execute. Measure twice, cut once. Measure, then pour. Pick your phrase. Proper planning is critical. Taken too far, you can land in analysis paralysis in planning your business. But shooting from the hip and hoping for the best is just as bad. Be decisive, not hasty.

Communications and Listening to Customers

Communicating with other people is hard. Even when we speak the same language, have similar backgrounds, and maybe even work in the same industry or company, everyone hears things differently. How we listen, how we interpret, and how we communicate is critical.

> Then Abram said to Lot, "Please let there be no strife between you and me, nor between my herdsman and your herdsmen, for we are brothers."
>
> **—Genesis 13:8**

Anyone ever heard of office politics? Guess it went back as far as Abram. Arguing over problems or turf accomplishes zero. Discuss the past only to learn from it, not to judge and chastise. Focus on solutions and move forward. One of the hardest jobs of the chief executive officer (CEO) is ensuring that the staff is in alignment and that they will do what they say they'll do. Ensuring honest, open lines of communication are in place is essential, and that has to start at the top of the organization.

> No longer do I call you slaves; for the slave does not know what his master is doing; but I have

called you friends, for all things that I have heard from My Father I have made known to you.

—John 15:15

Just for the record, let's not call our employees slaves. Aside from the wording, this is a good part of scripture to learn from. Keeping the front line involved with the direction and how you are doing in regard to goals is critical. When you conduct employee surveys or have town hall meetings, have you ever had anyone stand up and say, "Management is communicating too much to us. We don't care about what is going on"? I don't think so. While you can't communicate everything, regular, thoughtful communications with those in the trenches is needed.

For every breach of trust . . . [he or she] shall pay double.

—Exodus 22:9

Trust and track record are two intangibles that are worth their weight in gold. The prior quote and corollary was around communicating to the troops; let's use this one to talk about communicating upward. Communicating only the good things or half-truths or no communications at all will land you in hot water sooner or later. Failure to communicate problems or events promptly or completely will create a lack of trust with your boss and will bite you. If you feel that you can't communicate bad news upward, either you are mistaken or you need to be working for a different boss. If you can't be open with your boss, whom can you be open with? I've often told subordinates, "I'm not going to eat your lunch for making a mistake, but I will eat your lunch for not communicating slips in time or issues that need escalation." Bad news doesn't age well. And with that fracture in trust comes other measures that slow progress down.

> Know well the condition of your flocks, and pay attention to your herds; for riches are not forever.
>
> **—Proverbs 27:23-24**

Customer retention and satisfaction: I hope you are measuring these two metrics, as they are the signs of a thriving or dying business. Are you asking your customers how they are doing, what you could be doing differently, and what needs are not being met? Maybe it's time to do so. Pay attention to your herds, or you won't have them for long.

Roles and Responsibilities

As leaders, we can get tired of hearing about unclear roles and responsibilities in our organizations. I mean, really? We need to further define roles and responsibilities again? The answer is *yes*! Having clarity to roles and responsibilities only makes your business more

successful and in shorter time. When roles and responsibilities are clear, people can communicate with each
other at an almost telepathic level.

> Arise! For this matter is your responsibility, but
> we will be with you; be courageous and act.
> **—Ezra 10:4**

"That's not my job!" "I'm waiting for John to do
that." "I'm still not sure if we should do that." Heard
these gems before? Yeah, me too. Being responsible and
acting, doing something, and getting the job done: Is
that really so hard to do? Boy, sometimes it feels like it.
Staff members need to be empowered (and have some
guts to act and smartly stretch sometimes); leaders need
to be clear and decisive. Remember, only actions take
the hill—that is, the best-laid plans never win the battle;
execution of plans wins the day. Take initiative, take
responsibility, be courageous, and act!

> His master said to him, "Well done, good and
> faithful slave; you were faithful with a few
> things I will put you in charge of many things,
> enter into the joy of your master."
> **—Matthew 25:21**

Again, we'll ignore the master/slave terms and
concentrate on the meaning. It doesn't matter what
level you are at. We all have a boss, and hearing "Well

done" from the boss feels awfully darn good. It doesn't even need to be accompanied by "and here is your bonus" or "here is a raise," just simply "Well done." You can skip the "and faithful slave" part; that is a little too much. But seriously, do you send thank-you notes? Do you recognize people regularly? One of the best CEOs I ever worked for always started out her weekly leadership call with a request for who deserves recognition from executive leadership for the week. Then one of us would write that person a personal note recognizing his or her work and efforts. Don't miss an opportunity to say well done.

> Now this I say, he who sows sparingly shall also reap sparingly; and he who sows bountifully shall also reap bountifully.
>
> **—2 Corinthians 9:6**

Invest in people, your staff, your family, and your community—you never know whom you'll be working with, for, or beside in the future. Short-term goals lead to short-term actions. Not investing in people, whether due to time or other constraints, is like cutting off the research and development budget in an engineering company. You shouldn't sacrifice long-term value for short-term gain. Sure, you could get 20 more e-mails done, have that meeting where you just need to stay informed, or maybe do some long-needed filing, but how about spending a solid hour with your best employee? Doesn't that person deserve some of your best, focused time? He or she is kicking butt and delivering; think how the person would appreciate and love a solid hour of attention and time. Now do that to many folks, internal and external. You never know when a planted seed will come back and be fruitful to you. Pay it forward.

Seeking Counsel and Direction

As the boss, your job is *not* to have all the answers but to find the right answers by eliciting others, seeking counsel as needed, and then providing direction. Nobody has all the answers, and we all need counsel from time to time.

> Without consultation, plans are frustrated, but with many counselors they succeed.
>
> **—Proverbs 15:22**

Do you have to be the person who thinks of everything, or are you the one who is willing to listen to other people's ideas and thoughts and learn from them? Most people say, "Of course, I listen to everyone." But do you really? Be honest and consider this. Many heads are better than one, right? More than likely, it's always wise to have someone else's eyes on something that you are working on to have some objective feedback. Example: I was working on a new value proposition for my consulting firm. I went to a professor from my graduate school days who is now a friend and continues to be a mentor. My mentor looked at my new value proposition and started out with "Your baby is ugly. Sorry." My response: "Ouch, that stings, but thanks." He went on to give me solid feedback. While I didn't enjoy it at first, it was what I asked for and needed. I didn't need a "looks nice"; I needed real-world feedback. I got it, listened to it, and made some modifications. Nobody likes to be told their baby is ugly, but the realist takes that counsel and moves forward.

> But let everyone be quick to hear, slow to speak and slow to anger.
>
> **—James 1:19**

For some of us, especially us extroverts or Myers-Briggs "ENTJ" leaders, this is tough. Picture this: Someone is pitching a PowerPoint deck to us. We are thinking: Get it, get it, move faster, go ahead! Then, four pages in, we begin to dissect and make recommendations before seeing all the facts and figures. For some this is how we think: We talk extraneously, with our hands, jump ahead, think out loud, and talk through things. Others are processors; they listen in full till the end, then render judgment. I advise trying an approach down the middle (i.e., give feedback throughout, don't hold it all till the end, have a discussion). But let others get through more than the title slide before you rip them apart. Listen first, speak second. That's hard for some executives, including me. You know your style and your tendencies; simply look for moderation and balance. Be "quick to hear."

> So Joshua ordered the officers of the people: "Go through the camp and tell the people, 'Get your supplies ready. Three days from now you will cross the Jordan here to go in and take possession of the land.'"
>
> **—Joshua 1:10–11**

Speak clearly. Clear orders; equal clear direction. After you give clear direction, step back and let the lieutenants execute; they don't need you to micromanage them.

Execution

Getting stuff done—have we talked about execution a couple times earlier in this book? The Bible is full of "execution" passages. A quote from Samuel Goldwyn states, "The harder I work, the luckier I get." Funny how that works.

> But refuse foolish and ignorant speculations, knowing that they produce quarrels.
>
> **—2 Timothy 2:23**

Okay, which is it? You just said, listen to counsel, get feedback; now you are saying ignore speculation? Yes.

I didn't say leadership and business strategy was easy. If it was, there would be a cookbook for it, and people like me would be out of a job. Look at the scripture again: "refuse foolish or ignorant speculations," not all speculations. Which ones are foolish or ignorant—that is the $1 million question and why you get paid the big bucks to lead. Listen to feedback, know when to debate feedback in public versus private forums. Refute that feedback that is nonsensical or lacking, else you waste time debating it for no purpose. As the leader, it is your job to sift through the chaff for the wheat.

> Every branch in Me that does not bear fruit, He takes away; and every branch that bears fruit, He prunes it, that it may bear more fruit.
> —**John 15:2**

Okay, this is a tough-love verse. Pruning—pruning in our business. If you have a product line that is not producing, if you have an individual who is not suited for the position, if you have technology that is antiquated or a supplier that is not delivering, it may be time to prune and part company. Don't fret; it may not be a good fit for them either. The fallacy in business pruning is that you think you may be deeply hurting the other person, supplier, or entity by pruning it. In actuality, you may be saving it by putting it in a different environment in which it will thrive. The person who needs a different seat on the bus or a different bus altogether may be happy to leave to do something that is a better fit for them; the product line that is unprofitable and outside of your core mission could be a welcome bolt-on addition to another company; the supplier who didn't even realize that he wasn't delivering learns from this wake-up call to be more competitive. Don't ignore these things. Take action. Doing so is likely to help everyone involved.

> Let no one deceive you with empty words.
>
> **—Ephesians 5:6**

We all know people who talk a good game. Somehow they always seem to find themselves in good graces yet they never seem to be responsible or accountable to deliver anything. Do you have a team of doers or talkers? Think about it.

> One who is slack in his work is brother to one who destroys.
>
> **—Proverbs 18:9**

Go to Chapter 5 on farming and read about hard work again. If you are slack in your work, how do you expect to succeed and what kind of example are you setting for your staff?

> I have fought the good fight, I have finished the course, I have kept the faith.
>
> **—2 Timothy 4:7**

This last scripture verse is about executing a good fight, a good close to this chapter. It's easier to set direction, put goals in place, monitor periodically, and move on to the next challenge. But we must see things through. This is the pot calling the kettle black, because I am not good at this. I am better at turning things over to others to manage after I have set direction. And that may be okay, if you have your team set up in that fashion. But you can't turn a blind eye at the 10-yard line and assume the ball will get into the end zone. You can't say, "I've coached you down to the goal line. Now get it in." See that the ball gets into the end zone.

Final Closing Point

If you have gone through this chapter or even skipped to the end due to an issue with religion or otherwise and are still saying, "I struggle with business corollaries and the Bible. After all, the Bible is not about business or how to make money," I agree; the Bible was not written as a self-help book for business success and lessons in how to make money. But, again, as the most published, most copied work in the history of the world, it is worth a look to find parallels and lessons to apply in business. I also subscribe to the fact that money is not evil. Some religions preach about the evils of money. I'd respond, "Yes, you can do evil things with money, but money in itself is not evil. You can do tremendous good with it."

I believe you will find many, many verses in the Bible about money but the condemnation comes when you hoard it and don't use it for good. Recently a friend of mine reminded me of the New Testament verse "It is easier for a camel to go through the eye of a needle than for someone who is rich to enter the kingdom of God" (Matthew 19:24). If you die rich and haven't shared in your blessings, you may have some questions to answer. If you believe in capitalism and in sharing your blessings, consider this saying by John Wesley, an eighteenth-century Christian theologian: "Earn as much as you can; save as much as you can; give as much as you can." If you can do this, I think you will have lead a life with integrity and meaning.

Summary

Conclusion. Whether you believe scripture was divinely written or written by humans is irrelevant in this discussion. The Bible talks of vision and planning, communications and listening, roles and responsibilities, seeking counsel and direction, and execution—all of which are applicable to business today and are worthy of reflection.

Gold nuggets you took away to share with your board of directors or your staff, or for personal reflection:

1. _____

2. _____

Additional Resources/Tools

The Bible, obviously. I'd suggest any version of the Bible you are comfortable with: King James Version, New Living Testament, whatever. Just open it up and reflect.

Meditation at work. Laugh if you want, but try it. Not just yoga or meditation before or after work, meditation *at* work. You can easily meditate and do some breathing exercises at work to relax you instantly. It only takes a few minutes, and it's amazing how we can recenter and be refreshed.

Those two are enough. If you need more, go back to the conclusion or the gold nuggets.

Chapter 7

Everything I Needed to Learn about Business Strategy I Learned . . . from *Shark Tank*

A dream doesn't become reality through magic; it takes sweat, determination, and hard work.
—Colin Powell

I know, there are a lot of reality TV shows out there, and most are not all that great or realistic. But I do find some of the shows interesting. Obviously I enjoy many of the competitive cooking shows discussed earlier, but I have one other favorite that's a dead ringer for this discussion: *Shark Tank*. This is an entertaining show that teaches some good business lessons. Yes, I know some of the episodes are scripted, there is certainly a good deal of showboating, and some aspects are simply not real. But it's good television, and there are some gold nuggets on business in there if you watch closely enough.

The premise of the show is simple: Entrepreneurs can come onto the show and pitch their business to five sharks (savvy investors and entrepreneurs in their own right). The sharks can decide if they want to invest in the presenter's company or be out of the deal. Some of the individuals who come on this show are pure dreamers, and they expect things to magically unfold for them. They have a dream but few plans. Others have a dream, but they know it takes work and they go after their dream with a vengeance. They have a passion, and they want to win.

Let's use *Shark Tank* in two different ways to show some business lessons learned. First, we'll look at normal questions the show gets to that we should consider in our own business evaluations; then we turn to a shark-by-shark breakdown of questions asked based on personalities.

Typical Questions the Sharks Ask All Presenters

• **What are the economics of the deal?** Normally a presenter will say something like "I'm asking for a $250,000 investment for 10 percent equity in my company," then pitch away. So first thing the sharks think is that the entrepreneur is valuing the total company at $2.5 million. Will I get my money back and make a return the sharks wonder? They continue to listen to the deal, but sometimes when the presenter has made a flawed valuation and is asking for too much investment for not enough equity, the sharks devour the bait and send the presenter packing. The sharks expect entrepreneurs to be business savvy, and that includes being financially savvy. This is an interesting exercise to ask your staff. If your company needed a significant investment in the business, how much equity would you give up to get that investment? When you get into large companies, if you are a division, you are competing against other internal projects for limited capital. In *Shark Tank*, you are competing for venture capital, and you have to offer up equity. How much equity would you be comfortable giving up, hypothetically, and how would you value your company if a venture capitalist asked? Could you substantiate that estimate?

• **What type of deal is it?** Aside from the financials, the sharks are trying to categorize what type of deal it is. Is this a straight investment, like buying a stock and waiting for a return? Is it a deal where a shark's specific expertise is needed? Is it a pure licensing deal where the shark and the entrepreneur may take the company/product and sell it off to a larger competitor that has more marketing, branding, distribution, and operational efficiencies? Use these questions when you are contemplating new or enhanced business lines or products:

- Do you want to simply invest in them?
- Do you want to get additional expertise in house to leap-frog the product and make it more valuable?
- Do you want to sell off the product line, either outright or get into a licensing deal?
- Is there another economic proposition?

The point here is that there are many types of deals, and you could consider doing multiple deals in parallel. There is no rule saying you can't or shouldn't have a thriving product line, AND a product you are receiving royalties on, AND a joint venture you entered into and are getting a profit-sharing chunk, AND a business you are dressing up to sell off all at the same time. It's called a portfolio. Every business and every product are at different stages of their life cycles, and you need to recognize that investment profiles and economics change for each product or business. Don't lump them all in the same category and treat them alike.

- **What is the product being sold?** Is this in any way patentable or differentiated from the

competition? If there is no patent, what is stopping
other companies from swooping in on this market? If it
is not differentiated, why would I want to invest in it?
Shark's respond, "I don't need to invest in you. I could
do this myself." Everyone likes to think their product is
special or different, but you really need to ask yourself
whether it *really* is different and how to differentiate it
from other competitors in the market. Here are some
killer shark responses to entrepreneurs from the show:

- "Your competitors in this market are huge.
  They'll crush you like a cockroach."
- "I'll go do that in China myself and at half
  the cost."
- "There are 10 other products like that in
  the market."
- "What are you doing? Why are you not
  selling this online (or in retail or through
  brokers)?"

 • **Profit and loss: What does it cost to make
a unit? What is your overhead, including cost of
customer acquisition? What is your profit mar-
gin?** Know your numbers or get dismissed quickly
from *Shark Tank*. I relate this to conducting a quarterly
earnings release call and getting questions from ana-
lysts. You better know your numbers and have some
solid answers. Chief executives who don't know their

numbers are dismissed as not paying attention to the details or not understanding the true economics of the business. Another issue in this domain is financial savvy. The no-nos of trying to grow too fast, not recognizing the need for enough capital to fulfill orders, taking lavish salaries when not appropriate, and making other poor financial calls get you thrown off *Shark Tank*. In the real world, these actions can kill your business outright. Good leaders simply must know their financial ins and outs and associated operational metrics.

• **Distribution: How are you distributing your product: Website, retail, other?** What are your future distribution plans, and how can this mix change? Distribution is huge in any business. Having multiple distribution channels and relationships is usually paramount. Some businesses seem to get caught up in one channel or another and ignore the rest. Think of what the Internet did for ordering consumer product goods and just about anything. It was a once-in-a-lifetime distribution game changer that has narrowed the gap between small and large companies and domestic and international companies. You may not want to begin with several distribution channels at once, but you should have a balanced plan with multiple avenues to maximize growth and spread out your risk profile.

• **Why are you doing this? What prompted you to do this? Is this a hobby?** Sharks press at the entrepreneurs to find their passion. They want to know if the entrepreneurs are in it for a quick buck or have a fire in their belly to drive their company and product to success. In corporate America, think about this as deciphering between strategic products and businesses versus products and businesses you added, created, or bought that really are not full businesses or are some-one's pet project that just don't fit the mission of the company. Asking if a product or business line "is real" and in the strategic best interest of the company is sure to send the originators into a coronary. I've been there. But you have to do it. You have to take some bets but prune out those that are not growing, not part of your strategic purpose, or outright don't come to fruition. Be a shark and ask yourself and your team, "Why are we executing on this product or business line? Should we consider doing something different with it?"

• **What is your and others' perspectives on this business?** Entrepreneurs sometimes pride them-selves on being independent and making it on their own steam. Bravo, I say. But that doesn't mean you shouldn't have wise counsel in your corner to bounce ideas off of and validate big decisions. Even if you are the big kahuna, the big cheese, the boss, the top dog, everyone needs advice, and the smart ones seek it. Some people who come onto *Shark Tank* clearly have no personal or business mentors or advisors. Yikes! You can get so close to your baby, your idea, your business that you lose perspective. Many times on the show, the sharks are providing some perspective to these entrepreneurs because the entrepreneur has gotten too close and lost some perspective. The same lesson can apply to you: Take a step back once in a while; consult with someone in the industry (knowledgeable with a deep understanding), outside the industry (no blinders or preconceived notions), or simply a seasoned executive or leader you trust (someone with perspective no matter the product or industry who knows the right questions to ask); and get regrounded.

Round 2: Shark Personalities

Now let's take a different view of this show and look at the personalities, or the sharks, who are asking the questions. I want to take this approach to determine where you see yourself. Which shark do you relate to the most? Do you approach a business strategy or deal asking the same three questions and missing some other aspects, or do you have a balanced approach? The way this show is scripted and set up, each shark has a sweet spot, although I'm sure they could be much more balanced if needed. Think about your own approach and your team—and consider at the end if you have a good balance when you are debating, planning, and executing on business strategy.

- **Robert Herjavec.** Robert is my favorite shark. He's the son of a migrant factory work who is now a technology mogul. He grew up on a farm and is the epitome of rags to riches. Robert has strong intelligence quotient (IQ), but I tend to think of him even more as having the most emotional intelligence (EQ) on the show. Robert understands the soft skills and intangibles and is very thoughtful. He typically looks for these key attributes and asks these questions first:
  - **Passion.** Are you passionate about your business or product?
  - **Leadership.** I am investing in you just as much if not more than the product or business. What type of leader are you, and can I trust you?
  - **Drive.** Are you willing to work hard?
- **Mr. Wonderful, Kevin O'Leary.** If you've watched the show you know Kevin is a no-nonsense, straight-numbers kind of guy. Okay, maybe he's a bit of a bottom feeder as his deals normally suck the life out of presenters, but he's trying to make a buck. Kevin knows his sweet spot and is totally driven by the numbers. Here are Kevin's standards questions and approaches:
  - **Hard numbers.** What are the sales, profits, cost per unit?
  - **Royalties.** Have you thought about and is this an opportunity for a licensing deal? That is, if it is

more of a product than a company, why not sell it off to a larger competitor and get a royalty on every unit sold and let them worry about the rest?

- **Interest.** How do my little soldiers (my dollars) come back to me with friends (returns on investment)? Tell me how I'll monetize this investment and it's not a sinkhole for more investment down the road.

- **Daymon John.** Daymon is the marketing and branding expert. He created a line of clothing and brand, FUBU, and took it to billions of dollars. Daymon is a fun guy. He is flashy and tries to hide his heart a bit in making deals. But when he gets excited by something—a product or a person—he lights up and jumps in early and hard. Daymon's top focus areas include:

  - **Marketing.** What is the market for your product, your marketing plan, and your fit with competitors?

  - **Efficiency.** What is your cost structure, and how can you lower it? (Damon normally pushes hard for lowest-cost manufacturing. As he himself is in the clothing and retail space, he typically wants to see items produced overseas for cost effectiveness.)

  - **Demographics.** What do your customers say about this? Why have you focused on a particular demographic?

- **Lori Greiner.** Lori is billed as the Queen of QVC, where she does massive business. She holds multiple patents on products and is a successful businesswoman. Lori tends to look beyond the obvious value or product or company and is good at thinking about how to apply that product or company in a different space to make it much larger. Lori initially asks:
  - **Intellectual Property.** Do you have this idea patent protected? Is it a product, process, or utility patent?
  - **Distribution.** Is this a retail play, and how will you take this to market?
  - **"Zero to Hero."** I'm looking for ideas that can go from "zero to hero." I want the big ideas and products that can apply to the masses, not any niches. Do you see this idea going to the masses?
- **Mark Cuban.** Mark was added to the original show to replace a less colorful shark, and he really stirs the pot from time to time. He is very outspoken, and he knows what he likes and doesn't let much stand in his way. I think Mark can also be a good example of a shark with a less positive trait. When his ego gets out of check, he can make poor choices, get caught up in action over the deal, and pay too much money for it. Having said that, Mark has been a pretty smart investor, so let's not throw too many rocks here. Mark initially cares about:

- **Experiential background.** He knows what he likes to get into and what he doesn't. He doesn't stray about from core competencies and core mission. If a product or business idea doesn't match within a market Mark is comfortable with, he is out immediately.
- **Determination.** Mark assesses for attitude towards hard work and wants to see evidence that others will work as hard as he does. When he was a kid, he sold garbage bags to raise money for sneakers. He wants to know if others are this driven.
- **Relationships—it's who you know that can help you.** Mark has a lot of relations, aka connections. He likes to be the deal maker to hook people up to people, to create the infamous $1 + 1 = 3$. "If I can't help you, I'm out."

To me, one of the best takeaways of this show and these individual sharks is balance. The sharks quickly cover many standard questions to be asked of any business or business strategy, and then they press into the second level of questions on strategy and numbers and ask deeper questions. Each shark asks questions in his or her respective sweet spot, and individually and collectively the sharks assess what the company is worth, if they would want to invest in it, and if they can add any value. As you think through the characteristics of the sharks, which one do you relate to the most? On your staff, do you have all of these personalities covered so you are getting to all the evaluation questions you should be considering in your business? Many businesses would be stronger if they ran like independent entities that had to justify their strategies succinctly to a venture capitalist.

Summary

Conclusion. Regardless of industry, business maturity, and competition or other factors and forces, there are core questions that every business must address. Think about the questions a shark would ask you about your business. Can you answer these questions succinctly on the fly? Would you be comfortable with your responses on national television in front of family, friends, and peers?

Gold nuggets you took away to share with your board of directors or your staff, or for personal reflection:

1. _____

2. _____

Additional Resources/Tools
   Watch any season and any show from these programs. You're bound to learn business lessons and be entertained.

Read Robert Herjakec's book *Driven* to get a little inspiration and learn from a true shark and smart businessman.

Read *Hope Is Not a Method* by Gordon R. Sullivan and Michael V. Harper. I enjoy this book, and the title states its essence. I list this resource here because I think when new products or businesses are being launched, there's a lot of hoping and not enough planning and doing.

Part III

TOOLS, RESOURCES, AND CONCLUSIONS

Part III contains additional information on business strategy and management and conclusions to our discussion. We all have our toolbox of favorite tools, methods, and models. In this summary, I offer some of my favorites over the years. Some I learned in MBA school and then adapted as a consultant or after unsuccessful sessions and designing, some are PDE (proudly discovered elsewhere), and some I made up along the way altogether or as variations.

Yes, I'm giving you my favorite tools and methods. Some would ask, Why give those away and tell people how you perform your consulting work? You are giving away your value proposition. Giving you these tools is like telling you the best facts in science. Yes, I call them the best because I've tried a lot. Unless you have the "art" skill to conduct meaningful sessions around these models, I'm not giving away any secret sauce—remember the art vs. science discussion. In the same vein, I also know that many others can and do successfully perform this type of strategy work every day. So if you find something you like and that resonates with you, take it for your own use and good luck to you!

Last, I'll close out this fireside chat on business strategy with a top 10 winning checklist for successful business strategy. Enjoy!

Chapter 8

The Strategy Toolbox and Other References

Experience: that most brutal of teachers. But you learn, my God do you learn.

—C. S. Lewis

There are two parts to this chapter. First are my lucky-13 models and methods. These are models and methods I have used repeatedly over the years in business strategy planning, execution, and monitoring. These have been used, tweaked, modified, reused, and enhanced. You can look at the list and think, "Yup, MBA 101 stuff." But I'd argue that there are some good basic models here that work in the real world. They don't need to be, and actually shouldn't be, overly complicated. Few executives have time to spend days or weeks learning new business planning models. Models need to be comprehensive but straightforward. The real work comes in facilitating and consulting with folks on the content and steering them to get the best information and strategic insights possible. I've found that having experience in using and adjusting these models for circumstances is just as important as the original models themselves.

Additionally, I offer my top 12 best business books list. You will likely see some old favorites, but if you see something new or strange, look and see if it's something you'd like to read. Better yet, ask your staff members which ones they have read. Consider assigning a little homework to revive and refresh some folks and their strategic-thinking muscles. Muscles that are stretched and used function better than those that are dormant. I hope you find some nuggets in both of these lists.

13 Lucky Models and Methods

The next 13 models are pretty straightforward. Business strategy models do not have to be extravagant or bordering on rocket science to be effective. The best models are simple and straightforward and used to stimulate thinking, capture ideas, monitor and measure execution, and challenge current plans.

1. **Seven S model of strategic readiness—McKinsey model.** This model is a great gut check to how a business is executing. If you don't know how to facilitate an evaluation of executional effectiveness, try walking through the seven Ss of strategic readiness and assess where you think your business may have some opportunities.

    a. **Staff Management.** This is the individuals and levels of management that are managing the strategic and tactical day-to-day tasks of the business. Do we have clarity in roles and responsibilities and a balanced team?

    b. **Style Leadership.** Does management have a shared, compatible, understood style with which we conduct business and operate as a group and treat our employees? Do we effectively embrace change, clarify strategic intent, and appropriately shape the organization?

    c. **Skills Management.** This represents the basic skills to our specific business and the basic block-and-tackle skills with which to run any business.

    d. **Structure.** Do we have the appropriate structure in place to run this business? That is, is it both effective/efficient and aligned so that we can meet our strategic objectives?

    e. **Systems.** This area covers the systems with which we run our businesses, to include: financial and management control systems, market/industry intelligence gathering and analysis, enterprise resource planning/material requirements planning, business systems, continuous improvement, process reengineering discipline and structure, reporting systems/tools/processes, approval/authorization protocols, and others.

f. **Shared values—culture.** Do we have shared, clear values and expectations that are communicated to all employees of our division? Do we promote and reward those values (i.e., are our recognition and reward systems tied to promoting these behaviors)?

g. **Strategy.** Do we have the strategies and action plans in place to reach and achieve our divisional and corporate goals?

2. **Five force SWOT analysis—adaptation of Michael Porter's Five Forces model.** I've taken Porter's model and modified it to be more comprehensive and a model within a model, so to speak. It can be complex to populate and review, but it paints an incredibly complete picture of the business. Porter's Five Forces model considers: internal environment, supplier, customer, substitutes/complements, and entry forces. If you then apply the SWOT model (strengths, weaknesses, opportunities, threats) within each of those five forces, you can identify a lot of information. Additionally, within the SWOT items, to stimulate thinking, you

can use these categories to generate factors within the following categories: technical, economic, social, global, industry, and government. This approach can be complex, but if the group is ready to go beyond basic SWOT models, this model is comprehensive.

3. **Strategies under Uncertainty model—McKinsey model.** I like this model when there is a lot of turbulence and uncertainty in the market and in the business. Through the three levels of this model, you identify risks and scenarios, strategic postures the firm could make, and specific actions that you intend on taking. One of the benefits of debating with your leadership teams the various range of scenarios is to have some sense of how a business should react in the event of these scenarios and to agree in advance what you'll do as a firm. This prior knowledge will enable you to respond nimbly rather than being caught flat-footed and having to debate actions after the fact.

  a. Risks
- **Clear enough future**
- **Alternate futures**
- **Range of futures**
- **True ambiguity**

  b. Postures
- **Shape the future.** Play a leadership role in industry.
- **Adapt to the future.** Win through speed, agility, flexibility.

- **Reserve the right to play.** Invest sufficiently to stay in the game but avoid premature commitments.

c. Actions

- **No-regret moves.** Positive payoffs in any scenario
- **Options.** Could be significantly positive or minimally negative
- **Big bets.** Focused strategies with big payoff potential

4. **Balanced Scorecards—Kaplan and Norton.** When Kaplan and Norton's "Balanced Scorecard" article first came out in 1992, there was a lot of commotion. It was a solid, meaningful work on how to measure your business with a collection of metrics, not just financial ones. The premises of "if–then relationships" and significance of finding "leading indicators" versus just "lagging result metrics" was invaluable. Since this introduction, there have been a lot of adaptations of and variations on the core model. My Balanced Scorecard version normally includes these categories: customer, growth/innovation, operational excellence, people, and financial. Then, within each category, I identify both leading and lagging indicators. Lagging indicators are really results or targets that you are striving for. Leading indicators are more like milestone markers predicting

if you'll hit your results or not; therefore, they are slightly more meaningful but often harder to measure and get data on. You can go overboard on metrics and have too many in this model, so you need to be careful and only identify the top two or three metrics in each category for leading and lagging. That alone adds up to 20 to 30 metrics. Rule of thumb: If you can't get your scorecard on one page, it is too complex.

5. **Life cycle/growth curve.** There are many variations to growth curves that you can use. I use this tool to discuss, plan, manage, and modify a complete product portfolio. My version looks at the traditional product/service phases of introduction, growth, maturity, and decline. In the maturity and decline phases, I like to introduce a leap-frog or rebirth category so as not to fall down the decline curve all the way to zero. Looking at your product portfolio, discussing where to place your products, in which phase, can lead to a spiriting debate, and that's good. It's amazing if you do this Delphi style and make everyone categorize items silently and independently, then review the results. The variation can be staggering. If it is varied, that is all the more reason to complete this work and get everyone on the same page. If you have a pretty good consensus of where products fall in the model, then proceed to figure out any imbalances and holes in the portfolio; that is, consider these

questions: Do you have too many products in decline and nothing new in the introduction phase? How should you leap-frog products that are moving into the decline phase? Do we have too many or too few products? All are great questions for your leadership team to debate.

6. **Hedgehog model—Jim Collins**, *Good to Great.* I like this model and the discussion of finding your sweet spot is invaluable. Collins uses a Venn diagram and asks these three questions in each circle about a business:

a. What are you passionate about?
b. What can you be world class at?
c. What is your economic engine?

The convergence of these three circles and these three responses creates your hedgehog strategy. What can you be better at than anyone else in the world? Disclaimer: Note that this discussion can cause vomiting, irritation, eye rolls, irritable bowel syndrome, headaches, thrown pens, stomping fits, and other acts of aggression. Please use cautiously! Seriously: The discussion can be spirited, but again, that is good because if you are not all in agreement, you need to go through this work to get on the same page.

7. **Six Thinking Hats model—Edward de Bono.** It's been some time since I read De Bono's book *Six Thinking Hats*, but I have created an entertaining

workshop out of the concept. The basis is that there are multiple thinking hats that you should wear so as not to be blinded by any one school of thinking. Each hat has a color and an associated thinking style:

- White—neutral, just the facts
- Red—gut feeling
- Black—logical negative
- Yellow—positive thinking
- Green—Creative
- Blue—Controller/Organizer of all hats

In the past, I've had people in the room put on baseball caps, one color at a time, for 10 minutes, then switch to the next color hat and associated thinking pattern. People have really gotten into it, once they get past the fact that they are going to muss their hair (the sacrifices leaders make!). I've used this method to validate strategies, executional plans, and validate merger and acquisition success. It's best used when you are getting a lot of anecdotal stories from your leaders and need to get to some core facts along with those passionate thoughts. This model allows the passionate thoughts (negative and positive) to be put out there but also to get facts on the table and have a more healthy dialog.

8. **Full PMP (Project Management Professionals) methodology via the Project Management Institute.** If you have not heard of the institute or the PMP certification, here it is in a nutshell: In

the world of project management, a PMP is like a certified management accountant (CMA) or certified public accountant (CPA) certification in the finance world. To secure the designation, you take an exam after achieving an experience level in project management and, upon successful completion of their written exam, you get your PMP certification. The methodology the PMI uses and promotes has actions in five phases: initiating, planning, executing, controlling, and closing. I have found this methodology to be comprehensive and logical without being overly burdensome, and would promote it as a tool to run any midsize to large projects.

9. **CMA (Certified Management Accountant) certification from the Institute of Management Accountants.** You're not just going to run out and get this certification; the exam consists of two four-hour parts. Ouch. I took it straight out of college with some peers while others took the CPA exam. I always saw more value in the CMA exam due to its breath of content compared to the accounting depth of the CPA. The CMA exam covers four areas: business analysis, management accounting and reporting, strategic management, and business applications. I promote this credential because I am a firm believer that anyone in an executive financial role benefits from a broad background in all these

areas, in addition to deep experience in finance and accounting.

10. **Obituary exercise.** Sounds a little morbid, I know, but I've seen it be very effective and it's simple to do. The exercise is simple; ask the group "What could happen today such that our company would be dead or out of business in five years? For some reason, people are able to think morbidly pretty easily, so it's an easy exercise to get risks on the table, then to establish contingency plans around those risks so that they do not come to fruition.

11. **Venture capitalist exercise.** Everyone wants to play big dog for a day, right? Doing this exercise is simply asking a question. Throw a stack of Benjamin Franklins on the table (counterfeit bills are fine) and ask: "If you had unlimited resources to spend on fixing our businesses problems, what would you fix?" Normally the response is predictable but also surprising. Aside from the long shots of "build a new facility," "give myself a raise," and "buy out all our competitors," after some meaningful thought the answers are usually predictable *and* they do not require much out-of-pocket cash. Sure, lots of things require cash resources, but many problems and opportunities within a business require more time, cooperation, coordination, and communication than anything else. If you don't believe

me, try the exercise with your staff. You may be very surprised.

12. **Parity line—Strativity Inc. exercise.** This is a solid discussion I first saw facilitated by a consultant from Strativity Inc., a company that provides training and consulting in the field of customer experience. The exercise really drives to what is value added versus what is a commodity. The key delineator is if a customer would be willing to pay additional money for your product because it goes above the parity line (imagine a triangle with a horizontal line going through the middle—anything above the line, in the small part of the triangle, is differentiated, anything below the line is more common in delivery and not differentiated). It can be frustrating if you struggle with identifying how you differentiate your product offering, but that is what needs to be solved, isn't it? Every business needs to evaluate if it is a commodity or if it indeed needs to differentiate. Of course if you can prove differentiation, you should be able to charge a premium, and that is the ultimate test: Would a customer pay more for your product than for one of your competitors' products?

13. **Failure modes and effects analysis (FMEA).** FMEA was one of the first systematic techniques for failure analysis. It was developed by reliability engineers in the 1950s to study problems that

might arise from malfunctions of military systems. An FMEA often is the first step of a system reliability study. It involves reviewing as many components, assemblies, and subsystems as possible to identify failure modes and their causes and effects. While doing this can be very intensive in a military or manufacturing situation, the model can be applied more basically in a services business as well. As a matter of fact, in one services company, I used this model directly with clients to show them what we had concerns about and who was responsible for those risks as we implemented their business. We discussed having some shared responsibilities and how we needed to work together to ensure those failure points did not come to fruition. It also showed clients our thoughtful and comprehensive thinking and planning for their project and that this was clearly not our first rodeo. Just as teams win games before they step on the field to play, businesses succeed in delivering value when they have thoughtfully planned.

Personal Top 12 Most Valuable Business Books of All Time

Why do I like these books? It's simple. The authors told me something I didn't know or I hadn't thought of before. They told me something in a way that it has always stuck with me. Or they gave me a model that I can use to further evaluate my own thinking time and time again. If you can take a gold nugget or two from any book, retain it, and access it at a later time when you need it, you are ahead of the game. Thank you to those authors who did just that for me. In alphabetical order:

1. *Authentic Leadership: Rediscovering the Secrets to Creating Lasting Value* by Bill George
2. The Bible
3. *Blue Ocean Strategy* by W. Chan Kim and Renée Mauborgn
4. *Competing for the Future* by Gary Hamel and C. K. Prahalad
5. *Execution: The Discipline of Getting Things Done* by Larry Bossidy and Ram Charan
6. *First Break All the Rules: What the World's Greatest Managers Do Differently* by Marcus Buckingham
7. *Geeks & Geezers* by Warren G. Bennis and Robert J. Thomas
8. *Good to Great: Why Some Companies Make the Leap . . . and Others Don't* by Jim Collins
9. *The Innovator's Dilemma: The Revolutionary Book That Will Change the Way You Do Business* by Clayton M. Christensen
10. *Made to Stick: Why Some Ideas Survive and Others Die* by Chip Heath and Dan Heath

11. *The Seven Habits of Highly Effective People: Powerful Lessons in Personal Change* by Stephen R. Covey

12. *Swim with the Sharks Without Being Eaten Alive* by Harvey B. Mackay

What else would make your list?

Who on your team could use a refresher with one of these books?

One Final Tool

I'd like to close this chapter with one of the greatest tools and reference points I have in my arsenal, my family. One piece of advice I've gotten along the way in business was to have a personal board of directors. The advice was that chief executives have a board that they go to to share results, seek advice, and ensure they are on the right path and to support them in general. Why shouldn't you personally have a board of directors that you go to for advice, counsel, and support? Consider whom you would put on your personal board of directors. I can tell you that while I may not have formally elected members to my personal board (I thought that may be overboard), I have a short go-to list of people I trust and respect, and I seek their advice on major moves I'm considering.

My immediate family are some of my best advisors. My wife, Michelle, a successful and intelligent businesswoman in her own right, is grounded and straightforward. She doesn't mince words, and if I can't get something by her, it's not going to fly in many boardrooms or conference rooms across the country. My son, Alex, has the mind of an innovative engineer. He is analytical and sequential in his thinking and is driven to solve problems. When I tell him of a venture, it blows my mind that he can pick out a piece I may have overlooked in the sequence. My stepson, Jake, is more artistic and thinks about the "experience" of things. This is a good balance, as I can get caught up in strategy and initiatives and forget about what customers will think and how they'll react. This is a reminder that emotional intelligence is critical. My daughter, Rachel, is my youngest, and her world is vast and boundless. She loves to travel and aspires to do many things with her talents. She is often my acid test. If I can't explain something to her in three minutes, I've lost her interest. Sounds like a lot of CEOs and investors, doesn't it? But it's a good lesson. If you can't hold someone's attention and explain things in a simple, straightforward way to keep them excited, you don't understand what your value proposition is and you need to reconsider how to explain it.

I go to other family members, personal friends, past professors, past and present colleagues, and others for sage advice as well. Every member of my personal board of directors brings something unique to the table with different perspectives, experiences, and beliefs. And I don't tell them enough that I love them for that. Thanks, guys!

Chapter 9

Winning Checklist: How to Succeed in Business Strategy

A man's true greatness lies in the consciousness of an honest purpose in life, founded on a just estimate of himself and everything else, on frequent self-examinations, and a steady obedience to the rule which he knows to be right, without troubling himself about what others may think or say, or whether they do or do not that which he thinks and says and does.

—Marcus Aurelius

An organization's ability to learn, and translate that learning into action rapidly, is the ultimate competitive advantage.

—Jack Welch

These quotes from a great ruler and a great leader are certainly words to heed. Let's keep them in mind as we bring our discussion to a close and draw conclusions in relation to both what we need to do individually and how we need to lead our teams. We'll get to the winning checklist, but let's start with some negatives and get them out of the way. Many times it's easier to think of the negative things that can go wrong, like the obituary exercise from Chapter 8, than it is to find the positives. It's human nature, folks. And, of course, the inverse of any negative list leads to a winning list, but repetition builds skill, so play along. Watch out for these failures:

- **Failure to understand the customer and your market.** Why are your customers buying, and are they getting what they really want? Does your business strategy address these questions with real market data, or are you guessing at what you think the market needs?

- **Inability to predict market turbulence, or, worse yet, ignoring it.** Remember the old SWOT (strengths, weaknesses, opportunities, threats) and Porter Five Forces model? If you are not paying attention to turbulence within and around your environment, you are asking for trouble.

- **Failure to communicate and coordinate at multiple levels.** Communicate with your executive team, your staff, and your front-line employees.

- **Failing to outline clear roles and responsibilities to achieve your business strategy.** It's so simple, yet so many people have role confusion. Take the time to clarify roles and responsibilities, especially when you have a large team and business as things can more easily fall through the cracks.
- **Failure to obtain executive team commitment and buy-in to the strategy; failure to obtain employee commitment by not communicating or having proper incentives and rewards in place.** Buy in and incentives: it's business 101 stuff, yet when we get busy, we forget about the basics. Don't forget!
- **Failure to formulate a plan and then to follow it.** Execution without a plan is like a rudderless ship; how do you know when you get to your destination? You don't need a 1,000-step plan, but have a directional map.
- **Failure to manage change as it arises and adjust your plan in a timely fashion.** Adaptation to changes and making decisions in the midst of battle is a requirement. Few plans are perfect; you'll need to adjust them. Have a plan in mind for how you'll manage changes and adjustments to plan.
- **Failure to apply leadership and management in the business.** Even with a plan in place,

a course plotted, the ship does not steer itself. You need to be at the wheel, leading the business through strategy and managing through execution.

- **Accepting form over context.** When you are spending all your time wordsmithing PowerPoint slides, you have missed out. We've all been there, but don't let it happen again. I learned this and how to deal with it in years 2 and 3 at a company where I facilitated the strategic planning process. Year 1 was a successful business planning year. We had a good plan, solid strategies, good metrics, and ongoing monitoring. The success of year 1 led to us to trying to trump the success and get fancy in year 2. We focused on form over content without realizing it. In year 3 we went back to the basics. Everyone submitted content in Microsoft Word or on a blank PowerPoint template. After the content was nailed, we formatted it and put it in presentation form. It was the best plan we ever did.

- **Failure to realize where your business is at in its life cycle and to adjust your process.** Sometimes you don't need a full-blown, new strategic plan. As a matter of fact, if you've done a good job the prior year, you should be refreshing that plan, updating strategies for new factors, and adding or deleting other strategies. Your process needs to adjust each year depending on the state of the business.

Winning Conclusions and Summary

I think the best way to close this book is to tie it all together and give you the *10 universal truths* of business strategy—at least from my perspective and as told by others via cooking, movies, farming, the Bible, and shark deals. I call these universal truths because I believe they are the core components of just about every business strategy I've ever seen, created, or been a part of. While different components are required in different doses and have various significances depending on business, industry, product life cycle, competition, and other factors, they are all required. *The secret to business strategy is simple:* Identify *the essential puzzle piece (the secret sauce) to your business's success*, create a plan *for success, then consult on and help your team to* execute *your plan into gold.* As the alchemists in the Renaissance looked for the secret elixir to turn metals into gold, you need to identify and maximize the secret sauce that is critical to your business to turn your business strategy into gold. You may be missing an entire puzzle piece, or you just may need to tweak a couple things. But to plan, execute, and win with your business strategy, you'll need to master the next 10 elements:

1. **Planning.** We have had a lot of discussion on planning. At the end of the day, shouldn't this be at the top of your list in relation to business strategy?

You need to have a plan, else you run by the seat of your pants and never know where you are going. Or as Stephen Covey would say, "You can really get good at climbing a ladder, but if it's up against the wrong wall, who cares?"

2. **Listen to your customers.** When you become so inwardly focused and feel you absolutely know what your customers want more than they do, it's time to step back and take a reality check. Talk to your customers . . . a lot! If anyone on your leadership team does not normally engage with clients because he or she has a back office or support function, get the person out on the road. Everyone, especially your full executive

team, needs to be in front of clients to understand customer needs and live the experience you are providing to them.

3. **Execution.** Remember the military analogy "The best plan in the world can't take the hill." Well, I've just repeated it for effect. Make a thoughtful plan, monitor against it, and execute, execute, execute.

4. **Communications.** More problems can be solved through communications than we'd like to admit. We all like to think we are good communicators, but the fact is, there is always room for improvement. Make sure you are communicating with your board, your executive team, your middle management, your front-line troops, your distributors, your suppliers, and, oh yeah, your customers!

5. **Passion and innovation.** If you don't put some passion into what you are doing, it's difficult to make it through the hard times. If you are not innovating in your business—product innovation, process innovation, business model innovation, distribution innovation, financial innovation—then you are stagnating. Don't wake up in 10 years and wonder why you never followed your passions and are stuck in some meaningless job. Follow your passions and fortunes will follow.

6. **Intelligence: IQ and EQ.** Your intelligence quotient, IQ, gets you in the door. You need it as table stakes. But emotional intelligence, EQ, takes you

from the middle of the pack to the top of the heap. Be disciplined, make good calls, but remember: The best leaders have high EQ to build solid relationships, have balance, confront issues with awareness, and handle change. They build teams that have roots like those of sequoia trees. The root systems of sequoias do not go very deep considering their massive heights, but their bond together and passing of nutrients to other trees in the network that are in need is tremendous. They are the ultimate team.

7. **Know your numbers.** Think of *Shark Tank* on this one. Don't know your numbers? Then you're out of the tank! Know your critical numbers and metrics. They should be second nature to you, not just to your chief financial officer.

8. **Roles & responsibilities and teamwork.** Clarity is king. Clear roles and responsibilities, similar to communications, solve and eliminate a multitude of issues. When roles are clear and teamwork is promoted and rewarded, abundant synergies and results will be your outcome. Invest the time to do this right, and monitor it constantly. One bad egg can be a cancer to your team. Don't let it fester. Deal with it; it's your job.

9. **Sweat the details and ensure your staff is doing so too.** Almost all great leaders sweat the details. They love to and they live to do so. This

doesn't mean being a micromanager. Hire good people and let them do their jobs. But you should not abdicate your responsibilities to lead and manage. You must set an example for your subordinates on what they should be paying attention to. Know your numbers, know the details, be on the floor and the front lines of your business. You'll be sharp, in the know, limit surprises, and have the admiration of your troops because they'll see you rolling up your sleeves.

10. **Sharpen the saw.** Remember the story of my dad and fishing? Find something fun, something that will energize you, replenish your spirit, stretch your thinking, feed the soul, and prepare you for your next battles. This is easy to put off and say you'll do it next week, next month, and next year. But the days, weeks, months, and years go by fast. Sharpen your saw. Doing this might be at the bottom of your list but it probably should be at the top because if you are not healthy, in good spirits, and learning new things, everything else goes to hell. So take care of yourself, invest in yourself, and have a little fun.

A Closing Song

I hope this book has provided some insights into business strategy and looks into pitfalls to avoid—and that it was moderately entertaining along the way. So let's close with some thoughts from a well-known song, "Winning" by Carlos Santana. Google the lyrics and sing the tune in your head. The composer writes of going through a crucible event, as many successful leaders do. In the end, he's *born again* and *ready to play the game and win again*. Sing it now! I'm winning!

As you are humming or singing this tune, consider this. Life is not a game, and you only get one chance at it. But games are a common analogy for life, and sometimes you do feel as if you are on stage. Whether it's chess, blackjack, or a simple roll of the dice, sometimes you get lucky, but many times winners make their own luck by being smart, looking ahead 10 moves, and doing the hard unglamorous work of preparation even before the game is played. If you are successful in being *consultative* and *facilitative* with your team in regard to business strategy from planning through execution and monitoring, you'll be singing "I'm Winning."

But more importantly, you and your entire team collectively, and in perfect harmony, will be singing.

"We're winning!"

About the Author

Patrick J. Stroh, CMA, is principal of Mercury Business Advisors, which provides management advisory services in business strategy, innovation, product development, and business turnaround situations (www.mercuryba.com). He sits on the board of directors for Vail Place, a Minneapolis-based agency supporting those with mental illness, and also on the board of the Institute of Management Accountants, which serves 70,000 finance professionals worldwide. Stroh holds a bachelor's degree

in accounting from Minnesota State University–
Moorhead and an MBA from the University of St.
Thomas in Minneapolis. He most recently held positions within UnitedHealth Group, including chief strategy and innovation officer, client experience officer,
president of consumer health products, and senior vice
president of business strategy. He also writes a column
entitled "Innovation Elixir™" for the *American City
Business Journals*, reaching 43 metro markets across the
United States.

When he is not consulting or writing, Stroh enjoys
numerous activities and hobbies. During the sum-
mers, he enjoys wake-surfing and water-skiing on Prior
Lake in Minnesota, as well as taking his wife, Michelle,
his children, Alex, Jake, and Rachel, and the rest of his
family and friends tubing and wakeboarding, and for
lake cruises throughout the summer and fall. When not
on the lake, he enjoys the solitude and relaxation of
motorcycle riding through the countryside. He is also a
wine enthusiast with a private 1,000-bottle wine cellar
and tasting room, and he unleashes his creative energy
via cooking, having received education on French
cuisines and techniques at the Le Cordon Bleu culinary arts school in Minneapolis/St. Paul.

Index